Advanced
Bookkeeping

Workbook

© David Cox, 2016.

All rights reserved. No part of this publication may be reproduced, stored in a retrieval system, or transmitted in any form or by any means, electronic, mechanical, photo-copying, recording or otherwise, without the prior consent of the copyright owners, or in accordance with the provisions of the Copyright, Designs and Patents Act 1988, or under the terms of any licence permitting limited copying issued by the Copyright Licensing Agency, Saffron House, 6-10 Kirby Street, London EC1N 8TS.

Published by Osborne Books Limited
Tel 01905 748071
Email books@osbornebooks.co.uk
Website www.osbornebooks.co.uk

Design by Laura Ingham

Printed by CPI Group (UK) Limited, Croydon, CR0 4YY, on environmentally friendly, acid-free paper from managed forests.

British Library Cataloguing in Publication Data
A catalogue record for this book is available from the British Library

ISBN 978 1909173 781

Contents

Also available from Osborne Books...

Tutorials

Clear, explanatory books written
precisely to the specifications

Wise Guides

Handy pocket-sized study and revision guides

Student Zone

Login to access your free ebooks and
interactive revision crosswords

Download **Osborne Books App** free from the App Store or Google Play Store
to view your ebooks online or offline on your mobile or tablet.

www.osbornebooks.co.uk

Introduction

Qualifications covered

This book has been written specifically to cover the Unit 'Advanced Bookkeeping' which is a mandatory Unit for the following qualifications:

AAT Advanced Diploma in Accounting – Level 3

AAT Advanced Certificate in Bookkeeping – Level 3

AAT Advanced Diploma in Accounting at SCQF – Level 6

This book contains Chapter Activities which provide extra practice material in addition to the activities included in the Osborne Books Tutorial text, and Practice Assessments to prepare the student for the computer based assessments. The latter are based directly on the structure, style and content of the sample assessment material provided by the AAT at www.aat.org.uk.

Suggested answers to the Chapter Activities and Practice Assessments are set out in this book.

Osborne Study and Revision Materials

The materials featured on the previous page are tailored to the needs of students studying this Unit and revising for the assessment. They include:

■ **Tutorials:** paperback books with practice activities

■ **Wise Guides:** pocket-sized spiral bound revision cards

■ **Student Zone:** access to Osborne Books online resources

■ **Osborne Books App:** Osborne Books ebooks for mobiles and tablets

Visit www.osbornebooks.co.uk for details of study and revision resources and access to online material.

Chapter activities

1 The accounting system

1.1 Fill in the missing words to the following sentences:

(a) The [＿＿＿＿＿＿＿＿＿＿] accountant is mainly concerned with external reporting.

(b) The sales day book is an example of a book of [＿＿＿＿＿＿] [＿＿＿＿＿＿].

(c) Sales ledger contains the personal accounts of [＿＿＿＿＿＿＿].

(d) Sales account is contained in the [＿＿＿＿＿＿＿＿＿] ledger.

(e) Income minus [＿＿＿＿＿＿＿＿] equals [＿＿＿＿＿＿＿].

(f) [＿＿＿＿＿＿＿＿＿] minus [＿＿＿＿＿＿＿＿] equals capital.

1.2 In an accounting system, which **one** of the following represents the most logical sequence?

(a) Book of prime entry; financial document; double-entry bookkeeping; trial balance; financial statements (final accounts)	
(b) Financial document; book of prime entry; double-entry bookkeeping; trial balance; financial statements (final accounts)	
(c) Financial document; book of prime entry; double-entry bookkeeping; financial statements (final accounts); trial balance	
(d) Financial document; double-entry bookkeeping, book of prime entry; trial balance; financial statements (final accounts)	

1.3 Write out the figures which make up the accounting equation (assets – liabilities = capital) after each of the following consecutive transactions (ignore VAT):

- Owner starts in business with capital of £10,000 comprising £9,000 in the bank and £1,000 in cash.

- Purchases office equipment for £2,500, paying from the bank.

- A friend lends £2,000, which is paid into the bank.

- Purchases machinery for £8,000, paying from the bank.

- Purchases office equipment for £2,000 on credit from Wyvern Office Supplies.

1.4 Fill in the missing figures:

	Assets	Liabilities	Capital
	£	£	£
(a)	10,000	0	....
(b)	20,000	7,500	....
(c)	16,750	....	10,500
(d)	....	4,350	12,680
(e)	17,290	....	11,865
(f)	....	6,709	17,294

1.5 The table below sets out account balances from the books of a business. The columns (a) to (f) show the account balances resulting from a series of transactions that have taken place over time. **You are to** compare each set of adjacent columns, ie (a) with (b), (b) with (c), and so on, and state, with figures, what accounting transactions have taken place in each case. (Ignore VAT.)

	(a)	(b)	(c)	(d)	(e)	(f)
	£	£	£	£	£	£
Assets						
Office equipment	–	5,000	5,000	5,500	5,500	5,500
Machinery	–	–	–	–	6,000	6,000
Bank	7,000	2,000	7,000	7,000	1,000	3,000
Cash	1,000	1,000	1,000	500	500	500
Liabilities						
Loan	–	–	5,000	5,000	5,000	5,000
Capital	8,000	8,000	8,000	8,000	8,000	10,000

2 Double-entry bookkeeping

Note: a set of photocopiable blank ledger accounts is printed in the Appendix of *Advanced Bookkeeping Tutorial*, and is also available in the Products and Resources section of www.osbornebooks.co.uk.

2.1 Fill in the missing words to the following sentences:

(a) A [   ] entry records an account which gains value, or records an asset, or an expense.

(b) In the books of a business, the [   ] side of bank account records money paid out.

(c) In capital account, the initial capital contributed by the owner of the business is recorded on the [   ] side.

(d) Office equipment is an example of a [   ] asset.

(e) The purchase of a photocopier for use in the office is classed as [   ] expenditure.

(f) Repairs to a photocopier are classed as [   ] expenditure.

2.2   The following are the business transactions of Andrew King (who is not registered for VAT) for the month of October 20-4:

1 Oct	Started in business with capital of £7,500 in the bank
4 Oct	Purchased a machine for £4,000, paying by bank transfer (BACS)
6 Oct	Purchased office equipment for £2,250, paying by bank transfer
11 Oct	Paid rent £400, by bank transfer
12 Oct	Received a loan of £1,500 from a friend, Tina Richards, paid into the bank
15 Oct	Paid wages £500, by bank transfer
18 Oct	Commission received £200, by bank transfer
20 Oct	Drawings £250, by bank transfer
25 Oct	Paid wages £450, by bank transfer

You are to:

(a)   Write up Andrew King's bank account.

(b)   Complete the double-entry bookkeeping transactions.

2.3 The purchase of goods for resale on credit is recorded in the accounts as:

		Debit	**Credit**	
(a)		Trade payables account	Purchases account	
(b)		Purchases account	Cash account	
(c)		Purchases account	Trade payables account	
(d)		Trade payables account	Sales account	

2.4 Unsatisfactory goods, which were purchased on credit, are returned to the supplier. This is recorded in the accounts as:

		Debit	**Credit**	
(a)		Sales returns account	Trade payables account	
(b)		Purchases returns account	Trade payables account	
(c)		Trade payables account	Purchases returns account	
(d)		Trade payables account	Purchases account	

2.5 For each transaction below, complete the table to show the accounts which will be debited and credited:

(a) Purchased goods, paying from the bank.

(b) Payment received for cash sales, paid into the bank.

(c) Purchased goods on credit from Teme Traders.

(d) Sold goods on credit to L Harris.

(e) Returned unsatisfactory goods to Teme Traders.

(f) L Harris returns unsatisfactory goods.

(g) Received a loan from D Perkins, paid into the bank.

(h) Withdrew cash from the bank for use in the business.

Note: ignore Value Added Tax.

Transaction	Account debited	Account credited
(a)		
(b)		
(c)		
(d)		
(e)		
(f)		
(g)		
(h)		

2.6 The following are the business transactions of Pershore Packaging for the month of January 20-8:

4 Jan	Purchased goods, £250, on credit from AB Supplies Limited
5 Jan	Sold goods, £195, a bank transfer (BACS) received
7 Jan	Sold goods, £150, cash received
11 Jan	Received a loan of £1,000 from J Johnson, paid into the bank
15 Jan	Paid £250 to AB Supplies Limited by bank transfer
18 Jan	Sold goods, £145, on credit to L Lewis
20 Jan	Purchased goods, £225, paying by bank transfer
22 Jan	Paid wages, £125, in cash
26 Jan	Purchased office equipment, £160, on credit from Mercia Office Supplies Limited
28 Jan	Received a bank transfer for £145 from L Lewis
29 Jan	Paid the amount owing to Mercia Office Supplies Limited by bank transfer

You are to record the transactions in the books of account.

Notes:

- Pershore Packaging is not registered for Value Added Tax.
- Day books are not required.

2.7   Enter the following transactions into the double-entry accounts of Sonya Smith:

20-6

2 Feb	Purchased goods £200, on credit from G Lewis
4 Feb	Sold goods £150, on credit to L Jarvis
8 Feb	Sold goods £240, on credit to G Patel
10 Feb	Paid G Lewis the amount owing by bank transfer after deducting a prompt payment discount of 5%
12 Feb	L Jarvis pays the amount owing by bank transfer after deducting a prompt payment discount of 2%
17 Feb	Purchased goods £160, on credit from G Lewis
19 Feb	G Patel pays the amount owing by bank transfer after deducting a prompt payment discount of 2.5%
24 Feb	Paid G Lewis the amount owing by bank transfer after deducting a prompt payment discount of 5%

Notes:

- Sonya Smith is not registered for Value Added Tax.

- Day books are not required.

3 Balancing accounts and the trial balance

> **Note:** a set of photocopiable blank ledger accounts is printed in the Appendix of *Advanced Bookkeeping Tutorial*, and is also available in the Products and Resources section of www.osbornebooks.co.uk.

3.1 Which **one** of the following accounts normally has a debit balance?

(a) Loan	
(b) Bank overdraft	
(c) Sales	
(d) Purchases	

3.2 Which **one** of the following accounts normally has a credit balance?

(a) Drawings	
(b) Capital	
(c) Cash	
(d) Premises	

3.3 Prepare the trial balance of Tina Wong as at 30 November 20-9.

	£
Bank overdraft	1,855
Capital	9,000
Cash	85
Office equipment	2,500
Purchases	2,419
Purchases returns	102
Sales	4,164
Sales returns	354
Trade payables	1,082
Trade receivables	2,115
Vehicle	7,500
Wages	1,230

3.4   The bookkeeper of Lorna Fox has extracted the following list of balances as at 31 March 20-1:

	£
Administration expenses	10,240
Bank overdraft	1,050
Capital	155,440
Cash	150
Drawings	9,450
Interest paid	2,350
Loan from bank	20,000
Machinery	40,000
Premises	125,000
Purchases	96,250
Sales	146,390
Sales returns	8,500
Telephone	3,020
Trade payables	10,545
Trade receivables	10,390
Travel expenses	1,045
Value Added Tax (amount owing to HM Revenue & Customs)	1,950
Wages	28,980

You are to:

(a)   Produce the trial balance at 31 March 20-1.

(b)   Take any three debit balances and any three credit balances and explain to someone who does not understand accounting why they are listed as such, and what this means to the business.

3.5 Fill in the missing words to the following sentences:

(a) "You made an error of [_____] when you debited the cost of diesel

fuel for the van to Vans Account."

(b) "There is a 'bad figure' on a purchases invoice – we have read it as £35 when it should be

£55. It has gone through our accounts wrongly so we have an error of [_____]

[_____] to put right."

(c) "Who was in charge of that trainee last week? He has entered the payment for the electricity

bill on the debit side of the bank and on the credit side of electricity – a [_____]

of [_____]."

(d) "I found this purchase invoice from last week in amongst the copy statements. As we haven't

put it through the accounts we have an error of [_____]."

(e) "I've had the bookkeeper from D Jones Limited on the 'phone concerning the statements of

account that we sent out the other day. She says that there is a sales invoice charged that

she knows nothing about. I wonder if we have done a [_____] and it should

be for T Jones' account?"

3.6 The following are the business transactions of Mark Tansall, a retailer of computer software, for the months of January and February 20-4:

Transactions for January

20-4

1 Jan	Started in business with capital of £10,000 in the bank
4 Jan	Paid rent on premises £500, by bank transfer (BACS)
5 Jan	Purchased shop fittings £5,000, paid by bank transfer
7 Jan	Purchased stock of software, £7,500, on credit from Tech Software
11 Jan	Software sales £2,400, paid into bank
12 Jan	Software sales £2,000, paid into bank
16 Jan	Purchased software £5,000, on credit from Datasoft Limited
20 Jan	Software sales £1,500 to Wyvern School, a bank transfer received
22 Jan	Software sales £2,250, paid into bank
25 Jan	Purchased software from A & A Supplies £3,000, paid by bank transfer
27 Jan	Wyvern School returned software £280, refund made by bank transfer
29 Jan	Sold software on credit to Teme College, £2,495

Transactions for February

20-4

2 Feb	Software sales £2,720, paid into bank
4 Feb	Paid rent on premises £500, by bank transfer
5 Feb	Purchased shop fittings £1,550, paid by bank transfer
10 Feb	Software sales £3,995, paid into bank
12 Feb	Bank transfer, £7,500, to Tech Software
15 Feb	Purchased software £4,510, on credit from Tech Software
19 Feb	Bank transfer, £5,000, to Datasoft Limited
22 Feb	Software sales £1,930, paid into bank
23 Feb	Teme College returned software, £145
24 Feb	Software sales £2,145, paid into bank
25 Feb	Purchased software £2,120, on credit from Associated Software
26 Feb	Software sales £4,150, paid into bank

You are to:

(a) Record the January transactions in the books of account, and balance each account at 31 January 20-4.

(b) Draw up a trial balance at 31 January 20-4.

(c) Record the February transactions in the books of account, and balance each account at 28 February 20-4.

(d) Draw up a trial balance at 28 February 20-4.

Notes:

- Mark Tansall is not registered for Value Added Tax.

- Day books are not required.

- Mark Tansall's accounting system does not use control accounts.

- Make sure that you leave plenty of space for each account – particularly sales, purchases and bank.

4   Financial statements – the extended trial balance

Extended trial balance format

A blank photocopiable extended trial balance is included in the Appendix of *Advanced Bookkeeping Tutorial*, and is also available in the Products and Resources section of www.osbornebooks.co.uk. It is advisable to enlarge it up to full A4 size. Alternatively you can set up a computer spreadsheet – but remember to allow for all the rows shown on the layout – they will be needed in later Workbook activities.

4.1   Which **one** of the following does not appear in the statement of profit or loss?

(a) Closing inventory	
(b) Purchases	
(c) Interest paid	
(d) Cash	

4.2   Which **one** of the following does not appear in the statement of financial position?

(a) Closing inventory	
(b) Sales revenue	
(c) Trade receivables	
(d) Bank	

4.3   The following trial balance has been extracted by Matt Smith at 31 December 20-3:

	Dr	Cr
	£	£
Opening inventory	14,350	
Purchases	114,472	
Sales revenue		259,688
Rent and rates	13,718	
Heating and lighting	12,540	
Wages and salaries	42,614	
Vehicle expenses	5,817	
Advertising	6,341	
Premises at cost	75,000	
Office equipment at cost	33,000	
Vehicles at cost	21,500	
Sales ledger control (trade receivables)	23,854	
Bank	1,235	
Cash	125	
Capital		62,500
Drawings	12,358	
Loan from bank		35,000
Purchases ledger control (trade payables)		14,258
Value Added Tax		5,478
Closing inventory – statement of profit or loss		16,280
Closing inventory – statement of financial position	16,280	
	393,204	393,204

You are to prepare the extended trial balance of Matt Smith for the year ended 31 December 20-3.

4.4 The following trial balance has been extracted by Clare Lewis at 31 December 20-4:

	Dr £	Cr £
Sales ledger control (trade receivables)	18,600	
Purchases ledger control (trade payables)		11,480
Value Added Tax		1,870
Bank		4,610
Capital		25,250
Sales revenue		144,810
Purchases	96,318	
Opening inventory	16,010	
Salaries	18,465	
Heating and lighting	1,820	
Rent and rates	5,647	
Vehicles at cost	9,820	
Office equipment at cost	5,500	
Sundry expenses	845	
Vehicle expenses	1,684	
Drawings	13,311	
Closing inventory – statement of profit or loss		13,735
Closing inventory – statement of financial position	13,735	
	201,755	201,755

You are to prepare the extended trial balance of Clare Lewis for the year ended 31 December 20-4.

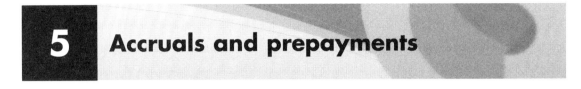

5   Accruals and prepayments

> **Extended trial balance format**
>
> A blank photocopiable extended trial balance is included in the Appendix of *Advanced Bookkeeping Tutorial*, and is also available in the Products and Resources section of www.osbornebooks.co.uk. It is advisable to enlarge it up to full A4 size. Alternatively you can set up a computer spreadsheet – but remember to allow for all the rows shown on the layout – they will be needed in later Workbook activities.

5.1   A credit balance at the start of the year on an expenses account indicates:

(a) A liability and an expense accrued	
(b) An asset and an expense prepaid	
(c) An asset and an expense accrued	
(d) A liability and an expense prepaid	

5.2   Which **one** of the following is an asset?

(a) Trade payables	
(b) Wages accrued	
(c) Bank overdraft	
(d) Income accrued	

5.3 This Activity is about ledger accounting, including accruals and prepayments, and preparing a trial balance.

You are working on the accounts of a business for the year ended 31 March 20-2. In this Activity you can ignore VAT.

Business policy: accounting for accruals and prepayments
An entry is made into the income or expense account and an opposite entry into the relevant asset or liability account. In the following period, this entry is reversed.

You have the following information:

Balances as at:	**1 April 20-1**
	£
Accrual for selling expenses	400
Prepayment for vehicle expenses	150

The bank summary for the year shows payments for selling expenses of £12,700. Included in this figure is £1,650 for the quarter ended 30 April 20-2.

(a) **You are to** prepare the selling expenses account for the year ended 31 March 20-2 and close it off by showing the transfer to the statement of profit or loss. Dates are not required.

Selling expenses

	£		£

The bank summary for the year shows payments for vehicle expenses of £7,200. In April 20-2, £280 was paid for vehicle expenses incurred in March 20-2.

(b)   **You are to** prepare the vehicle expenses account for the year ended 31 March 20-2 and close it off by showing the transfer to the statement of profit or loss. Include dates.

Vehicle expenses

		£			£

You have the following extract of balances from the general ledger.

(c)   **Using your answers** to (a) and (b), and the figures given below, enter amounts in the appropriate debit or credit column for the accounts shown. Do not enter zeros in unused column cells.

Extract from trial balance as at 31 March 20-2

Account	£	Dr £	Cr £
Accrued expenses			
Capital	45,000		
Discounts allowed	470		
Drawings	12,500		
Interest paid	380		
Office equipment at cost	24,500		
Prepaid expenses			
Purchases returns	2,740		

5.4   The following trial balance has been extracted by Cindy Hayward, who runs a delicatessen shop, at 30 June 20-4:

	Dr £	Cr £
Capital		90,932
Drawings	10,000	
Purchases	148,500	
Sales revenue		210,900
Repairs to buildings	848	
Vehicles at cost	15,000	
Vehicle expenses	1,540	
Land and buildings at cost	185,000	
Loan from bank		110,000
Bank	540	
Shop fittings at cost	12,560	
Wages	30,280	
Discounts allowed	135	
Discounts received		1,319
Rates and insurance	2,690	
Sales ledger control	3,175	
Purchases ledger control		8,295
Heating and lighting	3,164	
General expenses	4,680	
Sales returns	855	
Purchases returns		1,221
Opening inventory	6,210	
Value Added Tax		2,510
Closing inventory – statement of profit or loss		7,515
Closing inventory – statement of financial position	7,515	
	432,692	432,692

Notes at 30 June 20-4:
- Rates prepaid £255.
- Wages accrued £560.
- Vehicle expenses accrued £85.
- Goods costing £200 were taken by Cindy Hayward for her own use.

You are to prepare the extended trial balance of Cindy Hayward for the year ended 30 June 20-4.

6   Depreciation of non-current assets

> **Extended trial balance format**
>
> A blank photocopiable extended trial balance is included in the Appendix of *Advanced Bookkeeping Tutorial*, and is also available in the Products and Resources section of www.osbornebooks.co.uk. It is advisable to enlarge it up to full A4 size. Alternatively you can set up a computer spreadsheet – but remember to allow for all the rows shown on the layout – they will be needed in later Workbook activities.

6.1   A car which cost £20,000 is being depreciated at 30 per cent per year using the diminishing balance method. At the end of three years it will have a carrying amount of:

(a) £2,000	
(b) £6,860	
(c) £13,140	
(d) £18,000	

6.2   A car is being depreciated using the diminishing balance method. The original cost of the car was £15,000. At the end of year three it has a carrying amount of £5,145. What percentage of diminishing balance is being used?

(a) 20%	
(b) 25%	
(c) 30%	
(d) 35%	

6.3 A machine cost £48,000 and has an expected total output of 70,000 units and residual value of £6,000.

Calculate the depreciation charge every year for the first three years of its useful life, based on the following production output.

	Output	Depreciation charge
Year 1	15,000 units	
Year 2	20,000 units	
Year 3	10,000 units	

6.4 A machine which originally cost £1,000 is sold for £350 (both amounts net of VAT). The machinery: accumulated depreciation account shows a balance of £620. This means that there is a:

(a) Loss on disposal of £380	
(b) Gain on disposal of £350	
(c) Loss on disposal of £30	
(d) Gain on disposal of £30	

6.5 The bookkeeping entries to record a gain on disposal of non-current assets are:

	Debit	Credit	
(a)	Non-current asset account	Statement of profit or loss	
(b)	Disposals account	Statement of profit or loss	
(c)	Statement of profit or loss	Disposals account	
(d)	Bank account	Statement of profit or loss	

6.6 This Activity is about recording non-current asset information in the general ledger.

- You are working on the accounts of a business that is registered for VAT.
- During the year an old machine was sold.
- The machine had been bought for £8,000 plus VAT (the VAT was reclaimed), as already shown in the machine at cost account.
- Two years' depreciation has been applied.
- Depreciation is provided at 20 per cent per year on a diminishing balance basis.
- The machine was sold for £4,800 plus VAT (at 20%), with payment being received into the bank.

You are to:

(a) Calculate the accumulated depreciation on the machine now sold:

Year 1	£
Year 2	£
Total	£

(b) Make entries in the accounts which follow to record the disposal of the machine, showing clearly any balance carried down or transferred to the statement of profit or loss.

Machine at cost

Balance b/d	£8,000		

Machine: disposals

Bank

(c)   Tick the relevant box to show whether there is a gain or loss on disposal of the machine.

gain	
loss	

6.7 The following trial balance has been extracted by the bookkeeper of Wintergreen Supplies at 31 December 20-6:

	Dr	Cr
	£	£
Premises at cost	120,000	
Premises: accumulated depreciation		7,200
Bank loan		52,800
Capital		70,000
Sales ledger control	11,900	
Purchases ledger control		11,500
Drawings	6,750	
Cash	150	
Opening inventory	4,200	
Office equipment at cost	5,000	
Office equipment: accumulated depreciation		1,000
Vehicles at cost	10,000	
Vehicles: accumulated depreciation		2,000
Bank		750
Sales revenue		194,850
Purchases	154,000	
Wages	20,500	
Sundry expenses	9,500	
Value Added Tax		1,750
Disposal of non-current asset		150
Closing inventory – statement of profit or loss		5,200
Closing inventory – statement of financial position	5,200	
	347,200	347,200

Notes at 31 December 20-6:
- Depreciate premises at 2 per cent using the straight-line method.
- Depreciate vehicles and office equipment at 20 per cent using the straight-line method.
- Wages prepaid are £560, and sundry expenses accrued are £500.

You are to prepare the extended trial balance of Wintergreen Supplies for the year ended 31 December 20-6.

7 Irrecoverable debts and allowance for doubtful debts

Extended trial balance format

A blank photocopiable extended trial balance is included in the Appendix of *Advanced Bookkeeping Tutorial*, and is also available in the Products and Resources section of www.osbornebooks.co.uk. It is advisable to enlarge it up to full A4 size. Alternatively you can set up a computer spreadsheet – but remember to allow for all the rows shown on the layout – they will be needed in later Workbook activities.

7.1   The accounts supervisor of the firm where you work has instructed you to write off the trade receivable account of T Neal as irrecoverable. Which one of the following entries will you make in the double-entry accounts (assume that the business does not use control accounts)?

	Debit	Credit	
(a)	T Neal's account	Irrecoverable debts account	
(b)	Bank account	T Neal's account	
(c)	Irrecoverable debts account	T Neal's account	
(d)	T Neal's account	Allowance for doubtful debts account	

Note: ignore VAT.

7.2   An increase in the allowance for doubtful debts will:

(a)	Decrease profit for the year	
(b)	Be recorded in the trade receivables accounts in sales ledger	
(c)	Decrease the bank balance	
(d)	Increase profit for the year	

7.3   The statement of profit or loss of a business has been prepared showing a loss for the year of £2,350. A reduction of £150 in the allowance for doubtful debts should have been made, and irrecoverable debts of £70 should have been written off. Loss for the year will now be:

(a)	£2,130	
(b)	£2,270	
(c)	£2,430	
(d)	£2,570	

Note: ignore VAT.

7.4 You are the bookkeeper at Enterprise Trading Company. The following information is available for the financial years ending 31 December 20-5, 20-6, 20-7:

	£
• Trade receivables balances at 31 December 20-5, before writing off irrecoverable debts	105,200
• Irrecoverable debts written off on 31 December 20-5	1,800
• 2.5% allowance for doubtful debts created at 31 December 20-5	
• Trade receivables balances at 31 December 20-6, before writing off irrecoverable debts	115,600
• Irrecoverable debts written off on 31 December 20-6	2,400
• 2.5% allowance for doubtful debts adjusted in line with the change in the level of trade receivables at 31 December 20-6	
• Trade receivables balances at 31 December 20-7, before writing off irrecoverable debts	110,200
• Irrecoverable debts written off on 31 December 20-7	1,400
• 2.5% allowance for doubtful debts adjusted in line with the change in the level of trade receivables at 31 December 20-7	

Note: ignore VAT.

You are to show the effect of the above transactions on the financial statements in the following table:

Year	Statement of profit or loss			Statement of financial position	
	Dr **Irrecoverable debts** £	Dr **Allowance for doubtful debts: adjustment** £	Cr **Allowance for doubtful debts: adjustment** £	Dr **Sales ledger control** £	Cr **Allowance for doubtful debts** £
20-5					
20-6					
20-7					

7.5 This Activity is about accounting for irrecoverable debts and allowance for doubtful debts and preparing a trial balance.

You are working on the financial statements of a business for the year ended 31 December 20-6. In this task you can ignore VAT.

You have the following information:

Irrecoverable debts to be written off:	£
Craven Traders	75
Harris and Co	110
P Mahon	55
Allowance for doubtful debts at 1 January 20-6	300

The balance of trade receivables (sales ledger control account) before irrecoverable debts are written off is £12,740. The allowance for doubtful debts is to be 2% of trade receivables after irrecoverable debts.

(a) **You are to** prepare the irrecoverable debts account for the year ended 31 December 20-6 and close it off by showing the transfer to the statement of profit or loss. Dates are not required.

Irrecoverable debts

	£		£

(b) **You are to** prepare the allowance for doubtful debts account for the year ended 31 December 20-6 and to show clearly the balance carried down. Include dates.

Allowance for doubtful debts

		£			£

You have the following extract of balances from the general ledger.

(c) **Using your answers** from **(a)** and **(b)**, record the adjustments on the extract from the extended trial balance. Do not enter zeros in unused column cells.

Extract from trial balance as at 31 December 20-6

Account	Ledger balances		Adjustments	
	Dr £	Cr £	Dr £	Cr £
Allowance for doubtful debts		300		
Allowance for doubtful debts: adjustment				
Irrecoverable debts				
Purchases ledger control		8,960		
Sales ledger control	12,740			
Vehicles at cost	20,000			
Vehicles: accumulated depreciation		11,200		
Wages	22,850			

7.6 The following trial balance has been extracted by the bookkeeper of Jane Jones, who sells carpets, as at 31 December 20-5:

	Dr £	Cr £
Sales ledger control	37,200	
Purchases ledger control		30,640
Value Added Tax		4,280
Bank	14,640	
Capital		50,500
Sales revenue		289,620
Purchases	182,636	
Opening inventory	32,020	
Wages and salaries	36,930	
Heat and light	3,640	
Rent and rates	11,294	
Vehicles at cost	20,000	
Vehicles: accumulated depreciation		4,000
Machinery at cost	10,000	
Machinery: accumulated depreciation		1,000
Sundry expenses	1,690	
Vehicle expenses	3,368	
Drawings	26,622	
Closing inventory – statement of profit or loss		34,000
Closing inventory – statement of financial position	34,000	
	414,040	414,040

Notes at 31 December 20-5:

- Irrecoverable debts of £2,200 are to be written off and an allowance for doubtful debts of 5% is to be created.

- Depreciate vehicles at 20% per annum and machinery at 10% per annum, using the diminishing balance method.

- There are sundry expenses accrued of £270, and rates prepaid of £2,190.

You are to prepare the extended trial balance of Jane Jones for the year ended 31 December 20-5.

8 The rules of accounting

8.1 **(a)** Explain the accounting concept of materiality.

(b) Describe three types of situation to which the concept of materiality is applicable.

8.2 Eveshore Electronics Limited imports electronic goods from the Far East and sells to retailers in the UK. The company has always valued its inventory on the FIFO (first in, first out) method. One of the directors comments that, because of the recent strength of the pound sterling against Far Eastern currencies, the price of imported electronic goods has been falling throughout the year. She suggests that the closing inventory should be recalculated on the LIFO (last in, first out) method.

Assuming that the price of electronic goods has been falling throughout the year, would the change:

(a) Increase profit for the year	
(b) Decrease profit for the year	
(c) Have no effect on profit for the year	

8.3 Jason is a colleague at the accountancy firm where you both work. He has been asked to help with the costing of a building project for a client. The project is to be built in the centre of the village where you know that Jason lives. There is much opposition by the village residents to the project.

Indicate the **two** ethical principles faced by Jason.

(a)	Integrity	
(b)	Objectivity	
(c)	Professional competence and due care	
(d)	Confidentiality	
(e)	Professional behaviour	

8.4   In upholding professional behaviour, indicate the **two** types of pressures that a bookkeeper might face.

(a)	Materiality	
(b)	Familiarity	
(c)	Integrity	
(d)	Verifiability	
(e)	Authority	

8.5   **(a)**   IAS 2 *Inventories* states that inventories are to be valued at [_____]

[_____] . (complete the sentence).

(b)   A business buys twenty units of a product in January at a cost of £3.00 each; it buys ten more in February at £3.50 each, and ten in April at £4.00 each. Eight units are sold in March, and sixteen are sold in May.

What is the value of the closing inventory at the end of May using FIFO (first in, first out) and LIFO (last in, first out)?

	FIFO	LIFO
£54		
£61		
£60		
£48		
£40		
£135		

8.6 YZ Limited is formed on 1 January 20-4 and trades in two products, Y and Z. At the end of its first half year the inventory movements of the two products are as follows:

20-4	PRODUCT Y		PRODUCT Z	
	Bought *(units)*	**Sold** *(units)*	**Bought** *(units)*	**Sold** *(units)*
January	100 at £4.00		200 at £10.00	
February		80 at £10.00	100 at £9.50	
March	140 at £4.20			240 at £16.00
April	100 at £3.80		100 at £10.50	
May		140 at £10.00	140 at £10.00	
June	80 at £4.50			100 at £16.00

The company values inventory on the FIFO (first in, first out) method.

At 30 June 20-4, the net realisable value of each type of inventory is:

> product Y   £1,750.00
>
> product Z   £1,950.00
> _____
>
> £3,700.00

You are to calculate the value of:

(a)   Sales revenue for the half year.

(b)   Closing inventory valuation at 30 June 20-4 for each product using the FIFO basis.

(c)   Amount at which the company's inventories should be valued on 30 June 20-4 in order to comply with IAS 2 *Inventories*.

(d)   Cost of sales for the half year in order to comply with IAS 2 *Inventories*.

8.7 A shop is valuing its inventory at the financial year end. The following information is available:

- Inventory at selling prices is £240,000.
- The sales margin is 40%.

What is the cost price of inventory for the shop's financial statements?

£ [   ]

8.8 A business is valuing its inventory at the financial year end. The following information is available:

- Inventory including VAT is £288,000.
- VAT is 20%.

What is the cost price of inventory for the business's financial statements?

£

8.9 Which **one** of these is an example of ethical behaviour by an accounting technician?

(a) Valuing inventory at the higher of cost and net realisable value	
(b) Valuing inventory in accordance with IAS 2 *Inventories*	
(c) Valuing inventory in a subjective way	
(d) Valuing inventory in order to maximise profits	

8.10 Which **one** of the following is revenue expenditure?

(a) Purchase of a computer for the office	
(b) Legal costs for the purchase of property	
(c) Cost of extension to property	
(d) Quarterly electricity bill	

8.11 Which **one** of the following is capital expenditure?

(a) Repairs to vehicles	
(b) Goods taken by owner for own use	
(c) Cost of materials used to extend the premises	
(d) Renewing the electrical wiring in the office	

8.12   Wages paid to own employees who have redecorated the office are:

(a) Capital expenditure	
(b) Debited to the statement of profit or loss	
(c) Debited to premises account	
(d) Credited to the statement of profit or loss	

8.13   Classify the following costs:

	Capital expenditure	Revenue expenditure
(a) Purchase of vehicles		
(b) Depreciation of vehicles		
(c) Rent paid on premises		
(d) Wages and salaries		
(e) Legal fees relating to the purchase of property		
(f) Redecoration of office		
(g) Installation of air-conditioning in office		
(h) Wages of own employees used to build extension to the office		
(i) Installation and setting up of a new machine		

9 Accounting for capital transactions

9.1 Which one of the following is an intangible non-current asset?

(a) Vehicles	
(b) Goodwill	
(c) Hire purchase	
(d) Premises	

9.2 Eveshore Enterprises is considering the use of hire purchase as a means of financing a new computer. Which of the following statements is correct?

(a)	At the end of the hire purchase period, ownership of the computer will be transferred from the finance company to Eveshore Enterprises	
(b)	A hire purchase agreement is the same as a finance lease	
(c)	At the end of the hire purchase period, the finance company will collect the computer from Eveshore Enterprises	
(d)	Eveshore Enterprises will have ownership of the computer from the start of the hire purchase period	

9.3   John and Sara Smith run a delivery company called 'J & S Transport'. They started in business on 1 January 20-2 with two vans which cost £16,000 each (paid from the bank). On 1 January 20-4, a further two vans were bought at a cost of £18,000 each (paid from the bank) and, on 20 March 20-4, one of the original vans was sold for £8,000 (paid into the bank).

Depreciation is charged at 25 per cent each year, using the diminishing balance method; depreciation is charged in the year of purchase, but not in the year of disposal.

The Smith's financial year end is 31 December.

You are to show the accounting entries (journal and cash book not required) to record the acquisition, depreciation and disposal of vans for the years 20-2, 20-3 and 20-4.

Notes:

- VAT is to be ignored.
- Use one non-current asset vehicles account for all vans, one depreciation charge account and one vehicles: accumulated depreciation account.

9.4   Jane Barnet runs a printing business called 'Speedprint'. She needs to buy a replacement printing machine at a cost of £60,000 – the old machine is worn out and is worth only £500 as scrap.

Speedprint's current summary statement of financial position is as follows:

	£
Non-current assets	150,000
Current assets	80,000
	230,000
Less Current liabilities (including bank)	75,000
	155,000
Less Non-current liabilities	40,000
NET ASSETS	115,000
Capital	115,000

Speedprint is a profitable business, but one that is short of cash – the bank overdraft is up to the limit and Jane does not wish to approach the bank to seek an increase in the limit. The non-current liabilities are loans from friends and relatives – Jane does not wish to ask them for further monies.

Suggest two possible funding methods that Jane should consider to finance the new printing machine. Briefly summarise the features of each funding method.

9.5 This Activity is about non-current assets. You are working for a business known as Marston Metals. Marston Metals is registered for VAT and has a financial year end of 31 March.

The following is an extract from a purchase invoice received by Marston Metals:

To: Marston Metals Unit 10, Sunnydale Estate Marston MR3 8JK	Invoice 4728 Machine Supplies plc Wyvern Road Eveshore EV2 1QL		Date: 17 June 20-5
Pressing machine	Reference AB347	1	2,500.00
Installation of machine		1	160.00
One year service contract		1	100.00
VAT @ 20%			552.00
Total			3,312.00
Settlement terms: strictly 30 days net			

Marston Metals paid the invoice in full on 30 June 20-5.

The following information relates to the sale of a van:

Registration number	AB03 TPJ
Date of sale	14 February 20-6
Selling price	£8,000.00

- Marston Metals has a policy of capitalising expenditure over £500.
- Vehicles are depreciated at 25% on a diminishing balance basis.
- Machinery is depreciated at 20% on a straight-line basis assuming no residual value.
- Non-current assets are depreciated in the year of acquisition but not in the year of disposal.

Record the following information in the extract from the non-current asset register on the next page.

- Any acquisitions of non-current assets during the year ended 31 March 20-6.
- Any disposals of non-current assets during the year ended 31 March 20-6.
- Depreciation for the year ended 31 March 20-6.

EXTRACT FROM NON-CURRENT ASSET REGISTER

Description/serial no	Acquisition date	Cost £	Depreciation charges £	Carrying amount £	Funding method	Disposal proceeds £	Disposal date
Machinery							
Moulding machine	12/08/-3	10,000.00			Cash		
Year end 31/03/-4			2,000.00	8,000.00			
Year end 31/03/-5			2,000.00	6,000.00			
Year end 31/03/-6							
Year end 31/03/-6							
Vehicles							
AB03 TPJ	11/06/-3	16,400.00			Cash		
Year end 31/03/-4			4,100.00	12,300.00			
Year end 31/03/-5			3,075.00	9,225.00			
Year end 31/03/-6							
AB54 PZE	01/01/-5	15,200.00			Part-exchange		
Year end 31/03/-5			3,800.00	11,400.00			
Year end 31/03/-6							

9.6 Martin Varsani, the owner of Martin Manufacturing, needs to replace an old machine which is worn out. The cost of the new machine is £6,000 and Martin expects it to have a useful life of five years.

Martin Manufacturing is a profitable business, but day-to-day cash is tight.

Which **two** of the following methods would you suggest to Martin to fund the new machine?

(a)	Cash purchase	
(b)	Purchase of 30 days' credit terms	
(c)	Bank overdraft	
(d)	Bank loan	
(e)	Hire purchase	

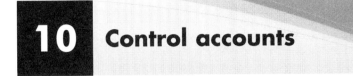

10 Control accounts

10.1 Indicate whether the following errors would cause a difference between the balance of the sales ledger control account and the total of the balances in the sales ledger.

Error	Difference	No difference
(a) Sales returns day book was undercast by £100		
(b) A credit note for £75 was credited to the account of Martley Traders instead of Martley Manufacturing – both are sales ledger accounts		
(c) The sales ledger account of C Fernandez, £125, has been written off as irrecoverable, but no entry has been made in sales ledger control account		
(d) A set-off entry for £45 has been incorrectly recorded as £54 in the sales ledger control account and in the sales ledger account		

10.2 On 31 December 20-6 the balances of the trade payables accounts in the purchases ledger of Thomas Limited were listed, totalled, and compared with the balance of the purchases ledger control account. The total of the list of purchases ledger balances amounted to £55,946. Investigations were carried out and the following errors were discovered:

(a) A purchases ledger balance of £553 had been listed as £535

(b) Discounts received of £100 had been credited to the trade payables account

(c) A credit note received for £141 had not been recorded in the trade payables account

(d) A purchases ledger balance of £225 had been listed twice

You are to record the appropriate adjustments in the table below; show clearly the amount involved and whether it is to be added or subtracted.

		£
Total of list of purchases ledger balances		55,946
Adjustment for (a)	add/subtract	....
Adjustment for (b)	add/subtract	....
Adjustment for (c)	add/subtract	....
Adjustment for (d)	add/subtract	....
Revised total to agree with purchases ledger control account		....

10.3 Prepare a VAT control account for the month of January 20-1 from the following information:

20-1		£
1 Jan	Credit balance b/d	6,240
31 Jan	VAT on purchases	11,046
31 Jan	VAT on purchases returns	498
31 Jan	VAT on cash sales	864
31 Jan	VAT on credit sales	18,347
31 Jan	VAT on sales returns	722
31 Jan	VAT on non-current assets purchased	1,845
31 Jan	Bank payment to HM Revenue & Customs	6,240

Balance the account at 31 January 20-1.

10.4 Prepare a payroll control account for the month of February 20-2 from the following information:

	£
• Wages expenses	17,342
• Bank payments to employees	11,367
• Pension fund liability	2,025
• Trade union fees liability	295

The liability to HM Revenue & Customs for the month is to be entered as the balancing figure.

10.5 This Activity is about preparing reconciliations.

The sales ledger has been compared with sales ledger control account at 31 March and the following points noted:

1   £120 of discounts allowed to trade receivables and entered in their sales ledger accounts has not been entered in sales ledger control account.

2   A set-off entry for £220 has been credited to the sales ledger account of Barker Limited instead of to the sales ledger account of Baker Limited.

3   In the cash book, the column for receipts from trade receivables has been undercast (underadded) by £100.

4   The account of D Doherty, £95, has been written off as irrecoverable in sales ledger, but has not been recorded in sales ledger control account.

5   A credit cale of £580 has been debited to the sales ledger account of Crossjoint Limited instead of to the sales ledger account of Crossways Limited.

6   A faster payment receipt from a credit customer for £745 for a debt outstanding at 31 March was received in April.

The total of the account balances in sales ledger is £24,275 debit and the balance of sales ledger control account is £24,590 debit.

Use the following table to show the **three** items that should appear in the sales ledger control account. Enter only **one** figure for each line. Do not enter zeros in unused cells.

Adjustment number	Debit £	Credit £

10.6 This Activity is about preparing reconciliations.

The purchases ledger has been compared with purchases ledger control account at 31 March and the following points noted:

1   The total column of purchases day book has been undercast (underadded) by £500.

2   A set-off entry for £190 has been omitted from purchases ledger control account.

3   A purchases return of £240 has been debited to the purchases ledger account of Spence Limited instead of the purchases ledger account of Spencer Limited.

4   £140 of discounts received from trade payables has been entered on the wrong side of purchases ledger control account.

5   A faster payment of £759 was sent to a credit supplier, but the amount that should have been paid is £795.

6   A faster payment to a credit customer for £1,054 was due on 31 March, but the payment was made in April.

The total of the account balances in purchases ledger is £18,790 credit and the balance of purchases ledger control account is £18,760 credit.

Use the following table to show the **three** items that should appear in the purchases ledger control account. Enter only **one** figure for each line. Do not enter zeros in unused cells.

Adjustment number	Debit £	Credit £

10.7 This Activity is about preparing reconciliations.

The bank statement has been compared with the bank columns of the cash book at 31 March and the following points noted:

1   Cheques totalling £1,210 paid into the bank yesterday are not showing on the bank statement.

2   A direct debit payment made by the bank for £360 has not been entered in the cash book.

3   A BACS receipt from a customer for £230 has been incorrectly entered in the cash book as £320.

4   Bank charges and interest of £120 have not been entered in the cash book.

5   A faster payment receipt from a customer for £258 for a debt outstanding at 31 March was received in April.

6   The bank made an error. On the last day of the month, a payment of £950 on the statement was duplicated.

The balance showing on the bank statement is a credit of £1,810 and the balance in the cash book is a debit of £4,540.

Use the following table to show the **three** items that should appear on the cash book side of the reconciliation. Enter only **one** figure for each line. Do not enter zeros in unused cells.

Adjustment number	Debit £	Credit £

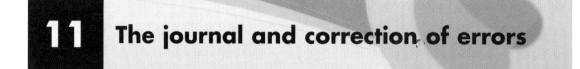

11   The journal and correction of errors

11.1   Which **one** of the following will not be recorded in the journal?

(a)	An irrecoverable debt written off	
(b)	Correction of an error of omission	
(c)	Closing inventory valuation at the year-end	
(d)	Bank payment to a trade payable	

11.2   The purchase of stationery, £25, has been debited in error to office equipment account. Which **one** of the following journal entries will correct the error?

	Debit		**Credit**		
(a)	Office equipment	£25	Stationery	£25	
(b)	Suspense	£25	Office equipment	£25	
(c)	Stationery	£25	Office equipment	£25	
(d)	Stationery	£25	Suspense	£25	

Note: ignore VAT.

11.3 A trial balance fails to agree by £27 and the difference is placed to a suspense account. Later it is found that a payment for vehicle repairs of £63 has been entered in the vehicle repairs account as £36. Which **one** of the following journal entries will correct the error?

		Debit		Credit	
(a)	Suspense	£36	Vehicle repairs	£36	
	Vehicle repairs	£63	Suspense	£63	
(b)	Suspense	£27	Vehicle repairs	£27	
(c)	Vehicle repairs	£27	Bank	£27	
(d)	Vehicle repairs	£36	Suspense	£36	
	Suspense	£63	Vehicle repairs	£63	

Note: ignore VAT.

11.4 What is the effect on the previously reported profit for the year of making adjustments for the following errors?

		Profit increases	Profit decreases
(a)	Sales account overcast		
(b)	Closing inventory undervalued		
(c)	Telephone expenses account undercast		
(d)	Discounts received omitted		
(e)	Depreciation charges for vehicles omitted		
(f)	Irrecoverable debt not written off		
(g)	Decrease in allowance for doubtful debts not made		

11.5   This Activity is about recording journal entries.

You are working on the financial statements of a business with a year-end of 31 March. A trial balance has been drawn up and a suspense account opened with a debit balance of £5,840. You now need to make some corrections and adjustments for the year ended 31 March 20-2.

Record the journal entries needed in the general ledger to deal with the items below. You should:

·   Remove any incorrect entries, where appropriate.

·   Post the correct entries.

You do not need to give narratives.

Do NOT enter zeros into unused column cells.

Ignore VAT.

(a)   Entries need to be made for an irrecoverable debt of £300.

Journal

	Dr £	Cr £

(b)   A purchase of office equipment for £4,000 has been made from the bank. The correct entry was made to the bank account, but no other entries were made.

Journal

	Dr £	Cr £

(c) No entries have been made for closing inventory for the year-end 31 March 20-2. Closing inventory has been valued at cost at £18,380. Included in this figure are some items costing £940 that will be sold for £700.

Journal

	Dr £	Cr £

(d) The figures from the columns of the purchases day book for 31 March have been totalled correctly as follows:

Purchases column	£4,600
VAT column	£920
Total column	£5,520

The amounts have been posted as follows:

Dr Purchases	£4,600
Cr VAT	£920
Cr Purchases ledger control	£5,520

Journal

	Dr £	Cr £

11.6 This Activity is about completing an extended balance.

You have the following extended trial balance. The adjustments have already been correctly entered.

Extend the figures into the statement of profit or loss and statement of financial position.

Do NOT enter zeros into unused column cells.

Make the columns balance by entering figures in the correct places.

Extended trial balance

Ledger account	Ledger balances		Adjustments		Statement of profit or loss		Statement of financial position	
	Dr £	Cr £	Dr £	Cr £	Dr £	Cr £	Dr £	Cr £
Allowance for doubtful debts		1,200	100					
Allowance for doubtful debts adjustment				100				
Bank	15,300							
Capital		30,000						
Closing inventory			25,230	25,230				
Depreciation charges			2,500					
Office equipment at cost	20,000							
Office equipment: accumulated depreciation		8,500		2,500				
Office expenses	12,700		500					
Opening inventory	22,680							
Payroll expenses	25,920			350				
Purchases	85,500		400					
Purchases ledger control		25,270						
Rent and rates	5,400			250				
Sales		151,200						
Sales ledger control	30,380							
Suspense	300		600	900				
VAT		2,010						
Profit/loss for the year								
	218,180	218,180	29,330	29,330				

Answers to chapter activities

1 The accounting system

1.1 **(a)** The **financial** accountant is mainly concerned with external reporting.

(b) The sales day book is an example of a book of **prime entry**.

(c) Sales ledger contains the personal accounts of **trade receivables**.

(d) Sales account is contained in the **general** ledger.

(e) Income minus **expenses** equals **profit or loss**.

(f) **Assets** minus **liabilities** equals capital.

1.2 (b) Financial document; book of prime entry; double-entry bookkeeping; trial balance; financial statements (final accounts)

1.3 • asset of bank increases by £9,000
asset of cash increases by £1,000
capital increases by £10,000
assets £10,000 – liabilities £0 = capital £10,000

• asset of office equipment increases by £2,500
asset of bank decreases by £2,500
assets £10,000 – liabilities £0 = capital £10,000

• asset of bank increases by £2,000
liability of loan increases by £2,000
assets £12,000 – liabilities £2,000 = capital £10,000

• asset of machinery increases by £8,000
asset of bank decreases by £8,000
assets £12,000 – liabilities £2,000 = capital £10,000

• asset of office equipment increases by £2,000
liabilities of trade payables increases by £2,000
assets £14,000 – liabilities £4,000 = capital £10,000

1.4

	Assets	Liabilities	Capital
	£	£	£
(a)	10,000	0	10,000
(b)	20,000	7,500	12,500
(c)	16,750	6,250	10,500
(d)	17,030	4,350	12,680
(e)	17,290	5,425	11,865
(f)	24,003	6,709	17,294

1.5 **(a)** Owner starts in business with capital of £8,000, comprising £7,000 in the bank and £1,000 in cash

(b) Purchases office equipment for £5,000, paying from the bank

(c) Receives a loan of £5,000, paid into the bank

(d) Purchases office equipment for £500, paying in cash

(e) Purchases machinery for £6,000, paying from the bank

(f) Owner introduces £2,000 additional capital, paid into the bank

2 Double-entry bookkeeping

2.1 **(a)** A **debit** entry records an account which gains value, or records an asset, or an expense.

(b) In the books of a business, the **credit** side of bank account records money paid out.

(c) In capital account, the initial capital contributed by the owner of the business is recorded on the **credit** side.

(d) Office equipment is an example of a **non-current** asset.

(e) The purchase of a photocopier for use in the office is classed as **capital** expenditure.

(f) Repairs to a photocopier are classed as **revenue** expenditure.

2.2   ANDREW KING

(a)

Dr		Bank account				Cr
20-4			£	20-4		£
1 Oct	Capital		7,500	4 Oct	Machinery	4,000
12 Oct	T Richards: loan		1,500	6 Oct	Office equipment	2,250
18 Oct	Commission received		200	11 Oct	Rent paid	400
				15 Oct	Wages	500
				20 Oct	Drawings	250
				25 Oct	Wages	450

(b)

Dr		Capital account				Cr
20-4			£	20-4		£
				1 Oct	Bank	7,500

Dr		Machinery account			Cr
20-4			£	20-4	£
4 Oct	Bank		4,000		

Dr		Office equipment account			Cr
20-4			£	20-4	£
6 Oct	Bank		2,250		

Dr		Rent account			Cr
20-4			£	20-4	£
11 Oct	Bank		400		

Dr		Tina Richards: loan account			Cr
20-4			£	20-4	£
				12 Oct	Bank
					1,500

Dr		Wages account			Cr
20-4			£	20-4	£
15 Oct	Bank		500		
25 Oct	Bank		450		

Dr		Commission received account			Cr
20-4			£	20-4	£
				18 Oct	Bank
					200

Dr		Drawings account			Cr
20-4			£	20-4	£
20 Oct	Bank		250		

2.3   (c)   **Debit**   **Credit**

Purchases account   Trade payables account

2.4   (c)   **Debit**   **Credit**

Trade payables account   Purchases returns account

2.5

Transaction	Account debited	Account credited
(a)	purchases	bank
(b)	bank	sales
(c)	purchases	Teme Traders
(d)	L Harris	sales
(e)	Teme Traders	purchases returns (returns out)
(f)	sales returns (returns in)	L Harris
(g)	bank	D Perkins: loan
(h)	cash	bank

2.6   **PERSHORE PACKAGING**

Dr	Purchases account		Cr
20-8	£	20-8	£
4 Jan AB Supplies Limited	250		
20 Jan Bank	225		

Dr	AB Supplies Limited		Cr
20-8	£	20-8	£
15 Jan Bank	250	4 Jan Purchases	250

Dr	Sales account		Cr
20-8	£	20-8	£
		5 Jan Bank	195
		7 Jan Cash	150
		18 Jan L Lewis	145

Dr	Bank account		Cr
20-8	£	20-8	£
5 Jan Sales	195	15 Jan AB Supplies Limited	250
11 Jan J Johnson: loan	1,000	20 Jan Purchases	225
28 Jan L Lewis	145	29 Jan Mercia Office Supplies Ltd	160

Dr	Cash account		Cr
20-8	£	20-8	£
7 Jan Sales	150	22 Jan Wages	125

Dr	J Johnson: loan account		Cr
20-8	£	20-8	£
		11 Jan Bank	1,000

Dr	L Lewis		Cr
20-8	£	20-8	£
18 Jan Sales	145	28 Jan Bank	145

Dr	Wages account		Cr
20-8	£	20-8	£
22 Jan Cash	125		

Dr	Office equipment account		Cr
20-8	£	20-8	£
26 Jan Mercia Office Supplies Ltd	160		

Dr	Mercia Office Supplies Limited		Cr
20-8	£	20-8	£
29 Jan Bank	160	26 Jan Office equipment	160

2.7   **SONYA SMITH**

Dr		Purchases account			Cr
20-6		£	20-6		£
2 Feb	G Lewis	200			
17 Feb	G Lewis	160			

Dr		Sales account			Cr
20-6		£	20-6		£
			4 Feb	L Jarvis	150
			8 Feb	G Patel	240

Dr		G Lewis			Cr
20-6		£	20-6		£
10 Feb	Bank	190	2 Feb	Purchases	200
10 Feb	Discounts received	10	17 Feb	Purchases	160
24 Feb	Bank	152			
24 Feb	Discounts received	8			
		360			360

Dr		L Jarvis			Cr
20-6		£	20-6		£
4 Feb	Sales	150	12 Feb	Bank	147
			12 Feb	Discounts allowed	3
		150			150

Dr		G Patel			Cr
20-6		£	20-6		£
8 Feb	Sales	240	19 Feb	Bank	234
			19 Feb	Discounts allowed	6
		240			240

Dr		Bank account			Cr
20-6		£	20-6		£
12 Feb	L Jarvis	147	10 Feb	G Lewis	190
19 Feb	G Patel	234	24 Feb	G Lewis	152

Dr		Discounts received account			Cr
20-6		£	20-6		£
			10 Feb	G Lewis	10
			24 Feb	G Lewis	8

Dr		Discounts allowed account			Cr
20-6		£	20-6		£
12 Feb	L Jarvis	3			
19 Feb	G Patel	6			

3 Balancing accounts and the trial balance

3.1 (d) Purchases

3.2 (b) Capital

3.3

TINA WONG
Trial balance as at 30 November 20-9

	Dr £	Cr £
Bank		1,855
Capital		9,000
Cash	85	
Office equipment	2,500	
Purchases	2,419	
Purchases returns		102
Sales		4,164
Sales returns	354	
Trade payables		1,082
Trade receivables	2,115	
Vehicle	7,500	
Wages	1,230	
	16,203	16,203

3.4   (a)

LORNA FOX
Trial balance as at 31 March 20-1

	Dr	Cr
	£	£
Administration expenses	10,240	
Bank overdraft		1,050
Capital		155,440
Cash	150	
Drawings	9,450	
Interest paid	2,350	
Loan from bank		20,000
Machinery	40,000	
Premises	125,000	
Purchases	96,250	
Sales		146,390
Sales returns	8,500	
Telephone	3,020	
Trade payables		10,545
Trade receivables	10,390	
Travel expenses	1,045	
Value Added Tax		1,950
Wages	28,980	
	335,375	335,375

(b)   See *Advanced Bookkeeping Tutorial,* Chapter 2 and page 45. The explanation should be appropriate for someone who does not understand accounting.

3.5

(a) "You made an error of **principle** when you debited the cost of diesel fuel for the van to Vans Account."

(b) "There is a 'bad figure' on a purchases invoice – we have read it as £35 when it should be £55. It has gone through our accounts wrongly so we have an error of **original entry** to put right."

(c) "Who was in charge of that trainee last week? He has entered the payment for the electricity bill on the debit side of the bank and on the credit side of electricity – a **reversal** of **entries**."

(d) "I found this purchase invoice from last week in amongst the copy statements. As we haven't put it through the accounts we have an error of **omission**."

(e) "I've had the bookkeeper from D Jones Limited on the phone concerning the statements of account that we sent out the other day. She says that there is a sales invoice charged that she knows nothing about. I wonder if we have done a **mispost** and it should be for T Jones' account?"

3.6   **(a)** and **(c)**   MARK TANSALL

Dr			**Bank account**				Cr
20-4			£	20-4			£
1 Jan	Capital		10,000	4 Jan	Rent paid		500
11 Jan	Sales		2,400	5 Jan	Shop fittings		5,000
12 Jan	Sales		2,000	25 Jan	Purchases		3,000
20 Jan	Sales		1,500	27 Jan	Sales returns		280
22 Jan	Sales		2,250	31 Jan	Balance c/d		9,370
			18,150				18,150
1 Feb	Balance b/d		9,370	4 Feb	Rent paid		500
2 Feb	Sales		2,720	5 Feb	Shop fittings		1,550
10 Feb	Sales		3,995	12 Feb	Tech Software		7,500
22 Feb	Sales		1,930	19 Feb	Datasoft Ltd		5,000
24 Feb	Sales		2,145	28 Feb	Balance c/d		9,760
26 Feb	Sales		4,150				
			24,310				24,310
1 Mar	Balance b/d		9,760				

Dr		**Capital account**			Cr
20-4		£	20-4		£
			1 Jan	Bank	10,000

Dr			**Rent paid account**			Cr
20-4			£	20-4		£
4 Jan	Bank		500	28 Feb	Balance c/d	1,000
4 Feb	Bank		500			
			1,000			1,000
1 Mar	Balance b/d		1,000			

Dr			**Shop fittings account**			Cr
20-4			£	20-4		£
5 Jan	Bank		5,000	28 Feb	Balance c/d	6,550
5 Feb	Bank		1,550			
			6,550			6,550
1 Mar	Balance b/d		6,550			

Dr		Purchases account				Cr
20-4			£	20-4		£
7 Jan	Tech Software		7,500	31 Jan	Balance c/d	15,500
16 Jan	Datasoft Ltd		5,000			
25 Jan	Bank		3,000			
			15,500			15,500
1 Feb	Balance b/d		15,500	28 Feb	Balance c/d	22,130
15 Feb	Tech Software		4,510			
25 Feb	Associated Software		2,120			
			22,130			22,130
1 Mar	Balance b/d		22,130			

Dr		Tech Software				Cr
20-4			£	20-4		£
12 Feb	Bank		7,500	7 Jan	Purchases	7,500
28 Feb	Balance c/d		4,510	15 Feb	Purchases	4,510
			12,010			12,010
				1 Mar	Balance b/d	4,510

Dr		Sales account				Cr
20-4			£	20-4		£
31 Jan	Balance c/d		10,645	11 Jan	Bank	2,400
				12 Jan	Bank	2,000
				20 Jan	Bank	1,500
				22 Jan	Bank	2,250
				29 Jan	Teme College	2,495
			10,645			10,645
28 Feb	Balance c/d		25,585	1 Feb	Balance b/d	10,645
				2 Feb	Bank	2,720
				10 Feb	Bank	3,995
				22 Feb	Bank	1,930
				24 Feb	Bank	2,145
				26 Feb	Bank	4,150
			25,585			25,585
				1 Mar	Balance b/d	25,585

Dr		**Datasoft Limited**		Cr
20-4	£	20-4		£
19 Feb Bank	5,000	16 Jan Purchases		5,000

Dr		**Sales returns account**		Cr
20-4	£	20-4		£
27 Jan Bank	280	28 Feb Balance c/d		425
23 Feb Teme College	145			
	425			425
1 Mar Balance b/d	425			

Dr		**Teme College**		Cr
20-4	£	20-4		£
29 Jan Sales	2,495	23 Feb Sales returns		145
		28 Feb Balance c/d		2,350
	2,495			2,495
1 Mar Balance b/d	2,350			

Dr		**Associated Software**		Cr
20-4	£	20-4		£
		25 Feb Purchases		2,120

(b)

Trial balance as at 31 January 20-4

	Dr	Cr
	£	£
Bank	9,370	
Capital		10,000
Rent paid	500	
Shop fittings	5,000	
Purchases	15,500	
Tech Software		7,500
Sales		10,645
Datasoft Limited		5,000
Sales returns	280	
Teme College	2,495	
	33,145	33,145

(d)   **Trial balance as at 28 February 20-4**

	Dr	Cr
	£	£
Bank	9,760	
Capital		10,000
Rent paid	1,000	
Shop fittings	6,550	
Purchases	22,130	
Tech Software		4,510
Sales		25,585
Sales returns	425	
Teme College	2,350	
Associated Software		2,120
	42,215	42,215

4 Financial statements – the extended trial balance

4.1   (d)   Cash

4.2   (b)   Sales revenue

4.3   EXTENDED TRIAL BALANCE

MATT SMITH

31 DECEMBER 20-3

Account name	Ledger balances Dr £	Ledger balances Cr £	Adjustments Dr £	Adjustments Cr £	Statement of profit or loss Dr £	Statement of profit or loss Cr £	Statement of financial position Dr £	Statement of financial position Cr £
Opening inventory	14,350				14,350			
Purchases	114,472				114,472			
Sales revenue		259,688				259,688		
Rent and rates	13,718				13,718			
Heating and lighting	12,540				12,540			
Wages and salaries	42,614				42,614			
Vehicle expenses	5,817				5,817			
Advertising	6,341				6,341			
Premises at cost	75,000						75,000	
Office equipment at cost	33,000						33,000	
Vehicles at cost	21,500						21,500	
Sales ledger control	23,854						23,854	
Bank	1,235						1,235	
Cash	125						125	
Capital		62,500						62,500
Drawings	12,358						12,358	
Loan from bank		35,000						35,000
Purchases ledger control		14,258						14,258
Value Added Tax		5,478						5,478
Closing inventory: statement of profit or loss		16,280				16,280		
Closing inventory: statement of financial position	16,280						16,280	
Profit/loss for the year					66,116			66,116
	393,204	393,204			275,968	275,968	183,352	183,352

4.4 EXTENDED TRIAL BALANCE

CLARE LEWIS

31 DECEMBER 20-4

Account name	Ledger balances Dr £	Ledger balances Cr £	Adjustments Dr £	Adjustments Cr £	Statement of profit or loss Dr £	Statement of profit or loss Cr £	Statement of financial position Dr £	Statement of financial position Cr £
Sales ledger control	18,600						18,600	
Purchases ledger control		11,480						11,480
Value Added Tax		1,870						1,870
Bank		4,610						4,610
Capital		25,250						25,250
Sales revenue		144,810				144,810		
Purchases	96,318				96,318			
Opening inventory	16,010				16,010			
Salaries	18,465				18,465			
Heating and lighting	1,820				1,820			
Rent and rates	5,647				5,647			
Vehicles at cost	9,820						9,820	
Office equipment at cost	5,500						5,500	
Sundry expenses	845				845			
Vehicle expenses	1,684				1,684			
Drawings	13,311						13,311	
Closing inventory: statement of profit or loss		13,735				13,735		
Closing inventory: statement of financial position	13,735						13,735	
Profit/loss for the year					17,756			17,756
	201,755	201,755			158,545	158,545	60,966	60,966

5 Accruals and prepayments

5.1 (a) A liability and an expense accrued

5.2 (d) Income accrued

5.3 **(a)** **Selling expenses**

	£		£
Bank	12,700	Accrued expenses (reversal)	400
		Statement of profit or loss	11,750
		Prepaid expenses	550
	12,700		12,700

(b) **Vehicle expenses**

		£			£
20-1 1 Apr	Prepaid expenses (reversal)	150	20-2 31 Mar	Statement of profit or loss	7,630
20-2 31 Mar	Bank	7,200			
20-2 31 Mar	Accrued expenses	280			
		7,630			7,630

(c)

Account	£	Dr £	Cr £
Accrued expenses			280
Capital	45,000		45,000
Discounts allowed	470	470	
Drawings	12,500	12,500	
Interest paid	380	380	
Office equipment at cost	24,500	24,500	
Prepaid expenses		550	
Purchases returns	2,740		2,740

5.4   EXTENDED TRIAL BALANCE

CINDY HAYWARD

Account name	Ledger balances		Adjustments		Statement of profit or loss		Statement of financial position 30 JUNE 20-4	
	Dr £	Cr £	Dr £	Cr £	Dr £	Cr £	Dr £	Cr £
Capital		90,932						90,932
Drawings	10,000		200				10,200	
Purchases	148,500			200	148,300			
Sales revenue		210,900				210,900		
Repairs to buildings	848				848			
Vehicles at cost	15,000						15,000	
Vehicle expenses	1,540		85		1,625			
Land and buildings at cost	185,000						185,000	
Loan from bank		110,000						110,000
Bank	540						540	
Shop fittings at cost	12,560						12,560	
Wages	30,280		560		30,840			
Discounts allowed	135				135			
Discounts received		1,319				1,319		
Rates and insurance	2,690			255	2,435			
Sales ledger control	3,175						3,175	
Purchases ledger control		8,295						8,295
Heating and lighting	3,164				3,164			
General expenses	4,680				4,680			
Sales returns	855				855			
Purchases returns		1,221				1,221		
Opening inventory	6,210				6,210			
Value Added Tax		2,510						2,510
Closing inventory: statement of profit or loss		7,515				7,515		
Closing inventory: statement of financial position	7,515						7,515	
Accruals				645				645
Prepayments			255				255	
Profit/loss for the year					21,863			21,863
	432,692	432,692	1,100	1,100	220,955	220,955	234,245	234,245

6 Depreciation of non-current assets

6.1 (b) £6,860

6.2 (c) 30%

6.3

	Output	Depreciation charge
Year 1	15,000 units	£9,000
Year 2	20,000 units	£12,000
Year 3	10,000 units	£6,000

6.4 (c) Loss on disposal of £30

6.5 (b)

Debit	**Credit**
Disposals account	Statement of profit or loss

6.6 **(a)**

Year 1	£1,600
Year 2	£1,280
Total	£2,880

(b) **Machine at cost**

Balance b/d	£8,000	Disposals	£8,000
	£8,000		£8,000

Machine: disposals

Machine at cost	£8,000	Machine: accumulated depreciation	£2,880
		Bank	£4,800
		Statement of profit or loss	£320
	£8,000		£8,000

Bank

Machine disposals	£4,800	Balance c/d	£5,760
Value Added Tax	£960		
	£5,760		£5,760

(c)

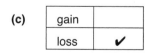

gain	
loss	✔

6.7 EXTENDED TRIAL BALANCE

WINTERGREEN SUPPLIES

31 DECEMBER 20-6

Account name	Ledger balances Dr £	Ledger balances Cr £	Adjustments Dr £	Adjustments Cr £	Statement of profit or loss Dr £	Statement of profit or loss Cr £	Statement of financial position Dr £	Statement of financial position Cr £
Premises at cost	120,000						120,000	
Premises: accumulated depreciation		7,200		2,400				9,600
Bank loan		52,800						52,800
Capital		70,000						70,000
Sales ledger control	11,900						11,900	
Purchases ledger control		11,500						11,500
Drawings	6,750						6,750	
Cash	150						150	
Opening inventory	4,200				4,200			
Office equipment at cost	5,000						5,000	
Office equipment: accumulated depreciation		1,000		1,000				2,000
Vehicles at cost	10,000						10,000	
Vehicles: accumulated depreciation		2,000		2,000				4,000
Bank		750						750
Sales revenue		194,850				194,850		
Purchases	154,000				154,000			
Wages	20,500			560	19,940			
Sundry expenses	9,500		500		10,000			
Value Added Tax		1,750						1,750
Disposal of non-current asset		150				150		
Closing inventory: statement of profit or loss		5,200				5,200		
Closing inventory: statement of financial position	5,200						5,200	
Accruals				500				500
Prepayments			560				560	
Depreciation charges			5,400		5,400			
Profit/loss for the year					6,660			6,660
	347,200	347,200	6,460	6,460	200,200	200,200	159,560	159,560

7 Irrecoverable debts and allowance for doubtful debts

7.1 (c)

Debit	**Credit**
Irrecoverable debts account	T Neal's account

Tutorial note: where control accounts – see Chapter 10 of the *Tutorial* – are in use, the credit entry will be to sales ledger control account.

7.2 (a) Decrease profit for the year

7.3 (b) £2,270

7.4

Year	Statement of profit or loss			Statement of financial position	
	Dr **Irrecoverable debts**	Dr **Allowance for doubtful debts: adjustment**	Cr **Allowance for doubtful debts: adjustment**	Dr **Sales ledger control**	Cr **Allowance for doubtful debts**
	£	£	£	£	£
20-5	1,800	2,585	–	103,400	2,585
20-6	2,400	245	–	113,200	2,830
20-7	1,400	–	110	108,800	2,720

7.5 **(a)** **Irrecoverable debts**

	£		£
Sales ledger control (Craven Traders)	75	Statement of profit or loss	240
Sales ledger control (Harris and Co)	110		
Sales ledger control (P Mahon)	55		
	240		240

(b) **Allowance for doubtful debts**

		£			£
20-6 31 Dec	Allowance for doubtful debts: adjustment	50	20-6 01 Jan	Balance b/d	300
20-6 31 Dec	Balance c/d	250			
		300			300

(c)

Account	Ledger balances		Adjustments	
	Dr £	Cr £	Dr £	Cr £
Allowance for doubtful debts		300	50	
Allowance for doubtful debts: adjustment				50
Irrecoverable debts			240	
Purchases ledger control		8,960		
Sales ledger control	12,740			240
Vehicles at cost	20,000			
Vehicles: accumulated depreciation		11,200		
Wages	22,850			

7.6 EXTENDED TRIAL BALANCE

JANE JONES
31 DECEMBER 20-5

Account name	Ledger balances Dr £	Ledger balances Cr £	Adjustments Dr £	Adjustments Cr £	Statement of profit or loss Dr £	Statement of profit or loss Cr £	Statement of financial position Dr £	Statement of financial position Cr £
Sales ledger control	37,200			2,200			35,000	
Purchases ledger control		30,640						30,640
Value Added Tax		4,280						4,280
Bank	14,640						14,640	
Capital		50,500						50,500
Sales revenue		289,620				289,620		
Purchases	182,636				182,636			
Opening inventory	32,020				32,020			
Wages and salaries	36,930				36,930			
Heat and light	3,640				3,640			
Rent and rates	11,294			2,190	9,104			
Vehicles at cost	20,000						20,000	
Vehicles: accumulated depreciation		4,000		3,200				7,200
Machinery at cost	10,000						10,000	
Machinery: accumulated depreciation		1,000		900				1,900
Sundry expenses	1,690		270		1,960			
Vehicle expenses	3,368				3,368			
Drawings	26,622						26,622	
Closing inventory: statement of profit or loss		34,000				34,000		
Closing inventory: statement of financial position	34,000						34,000	
Accruals				270				270
Prepayments			2,190				2,190	
Depreciation charges			4,100		4,100			
Irrecoverable debts			2,200		2,200			
Allowance for doubtful debts				1,750				1,750
Allowance for doubtful debts: adjustment			1,750		1,750			
Profit/loss for the year					45,912			45,912
	414,040	414,040	10,510	10,510	323,620	323,620	142,452	142,452

8 The rules of accounting

8.1 **(a)** The accounting concept of materiality means that some items in accounts are of such a low monetary value that it is not worthwhile recording them separately, ie they are not 'material'.

(b) • Small expense items do not justify their own separate expense account; instead they are grouped together in a sundry expenses account.

• End-of-year unused office stationery is often not valued for the purpose of financial statements, because the amount is not material and does not justify the time and effort involved.

• Low-cost non-current assets are often charged as an expense in the statement of profit or loss, instead of being classed as capital expenditure.

8.2 (a) Increase profit for the year.

Tutorial notes:
• With falling prices,
    – FIFO gives a lower closing inventory valuation (because the closing inventory consists of the most recently purchased items)
    – LIFO gives a higher closing inventory valuation (because the closing inventory consists of the oldest purchased items)

• In this year's statement of profit or loss, cost of sales will be:
    – higher under FIFO, giving a lower profit
    – lower under LIFO, giving a higher profit

• This year's closing inventory valuation will affect next year's profit – over the life of a business, total profit is the same whichever method of inventory valuation is used.

8.3 (d) Confidentiality, and (e) Professional behaviour

8.4 (b) Familiarity, and (e) Authority

8.5 (a) IAS 2 *Inventories* states that inventories are to be valued at **the lower of cost and net realisable value.**

(b)

	FIFO	LIFO
£54		
£61	✔	
£60		
£48		✔
£40		
£135		

Tutorial notes:

The closing inventory is:

	units bought (20 + 10 + 10)	=	40
less	units sold (8 + 16)	=	24
equals	closing inventory	=	16

(a) FIFO

	6 units at £3.50	=	£21.00
	10 units at £4.00	=	£40.00
	16 units	=	£61.00

(b) LIFO

	16 units at £3.00	=	£48.00

8.6   **(a)**   Sales revenue for the half year: £

·   product Y, 220 units at £10.00 each   =   2,200.00

·   product Z, 340 units at £16.00 each   =   5,440.00

·   total sales   =   <u>7,640.00</u>

(b)   Product Y: £

20 units at £4.20 per unit   =   84.00

100 units at £3.80 per unit   =   380.00

80 units at £4.50 per unit   =   <u>360.00</u>

200 units   =   <u>824.00</u>

Product Z: £

60 units at £10.50 per unit   =   630.00

140 units at £10.00 per unit   =   <u>1,400.00</u>

200 units   =   <u>2,030.00</u>

(c)   £

·   Product Y   =   824.00   (cost price)

·   Product Z   =   <u>1,950.00</u>   (net realisable value)

                                   <u>2,774.00</u>

(d)   Purchases   £

·   product Y   =   1,728.00

·   product Z   =   <u>5,400.00</u>

                                   7,128.00

Less closing inventory   =   <u>2,774.00</u>

Cost of sales   <u>4,354.00</u>

8.7   £144,000, ie £240,000 x (100 − 40)/100

8.8   £240,000, ie £288,000 x 100/(100 + 20)

8.9   (b)   Valuing inventory in accordance with IAS 2 *Inventories*

8.10 (d)   Quarterly electricity bill

8.11 (c)   Cost of materials used to extend the premises

8.12 (b)   Debited to the statement of profit or loss

8.13

		Capital expenditure	Revenue expenditure
(a)	Purchase of vehicles	✔	
(b)	Depreciation of vehicles		✔
(c)	Rent paid on premises		✔
(d)	Wages and salaries		✔
(e)	Legal fees relating to the purchase of property	✔	
(f)	Redecoration of office		✔
(g)	Installation of air-conditioning in office	✔	
(h)	Wages of own employees used to build extension to the office	✔	
(i)	Installation and setting up of a new machine	✔	

9 Accounting for capital transactions

9.1 (b) Goodwill

9.2 (a) At the end of the hire purchase period, ownership of the computer will be transferred from the finance company to Eveshore Enterprises.

9.3 **Depreciation calculations:**

	20-2	20-3	20-4	Total
	£	£	£	£
Van 1	4,000	3,000	–	7,000
Van 2	4,000	3,000	2,250	9,250
Van 3	–	–	4,500	4,500
Van 4	–	–	4,500	4,500
Total	8,000	6,000	11,250	25,250

Dr		Vehicles at cost account			Cr
20-2			£	20-2		£
01 Jan	Bank	16,000	31 Dec	Balance c/d	32,000
01 Jan	Bank	16,000			
		32,000			32,000
20-3				20-3		
01 Jan	Balance b/d	32,000	31 Dec	Balance c/d	32,000
20-4				20-4		
01 Jan	Balance b/d	32,000	20 Mar	Disposals	16,000
01 Jan	Bank	18,000	31 Dec	Balance c/d	52,000
01 Jan	Bank	18,000			
		68,000			68,000
20-5				20-5		
01 Jan	Balance b/d	52,000			

Dr	Depreciation charges account			Cr
20-2		£	20-2		£
31 Dec Vehicles: accumulated depreciation	8,000	31 Dec Statement of profit or loss	8,000
20-3			20-3		
31 Dec Vehicles: accumulated depreciation	6,000	31 Dec Statement of profit or loss	6,000
20-4			20-4		
31 Dec Vehicles: accumulated depreciation	11,250	31 Dec Statement of profit or loss	11,250

Dr		Vehicles: accumulated depreciation account			Cr
20-2		£	20-2		£
31 Dec	Balance c/d	8,000	31 Dec	Depreciation charges	8,000
20-3			20-3		
31 Dec	Balance c/d	14,000	01 Jan	Balance b/d	8,000
			31 Dec	Depreciation charges	6,000
		14,000			14,000
20-4			20-4		
20 Mar	Disposals	7,000	01 Jan	Balance b/d	14,000
31 Dec	Balance c/d	18,250	31 Dec	Depreciation charges	11,250
		25,250			25,250
20-5			20-5		
			01 Jan	Balance b/d	18,250

Dr		Vehicle disposals account			Cr
20-4		£	20-4		£
20 Mar	Vehicles	16,000	20 Mar	Vehicles: accumulated depreciation	7,000
			20 Mar	Bank	8,000
			20 Mar	Statement of profit or loss (loss on disposal)	1,000
		16,000			16,000

9.4 Jane should consider:
*   hire purchase
*   a finance lease

Hire purchase

*   An agreement with a finance company which will enable Speedprint (the hirer) to have the use of the new printing machine on payment of a deposit.
*   The finance company owns the printing machine and Speedprint will make regular instalment payments – monthly, quarterly or half-yearly – which will pay back the cost plus interest over a set period.
*   At the end of the hire purchase period, ownership of the printing machine will pass from the finance company to Speedprint.

Finance lease

*   An agreement whereby Speedprint (the lessee) has the use of the printing machine, which is owned by a finance company (the lessor).
*   Speedprint will make regular rental payments to the lessor over the period of the lease, which might be up to seven years.
*   There is normally no provision in a finance lease for legal ownership of the leased asset to pass to the lessee at the end of the lease.

9.5

EXTRACT FROM NON-CURRENT ASSET REGISTER							
Description/serial no	Acquisition date	Cost £	Depreciation charges £	Carrying amount £	Funding method	Disposal proceeds £	Disposal date
Machinery							
Moulding machine	12/08/-3	10,000.00			Cash		
Year end 31/03/-4			2,000.00	8,000.00			
Year end 31/03/-5			2,000.00	6,000.00			
Year end 31/03/-6			2,000.00	4,000.00			
Pressing machine	17/06/-5	2,660.00			Cash		
Year end 31/03/-6			532.00	2,128.00			
Vehicles							
AB03 TPJ	11/06/-3	16,400.00			Cash		
Year end 31/03/-4			4,100.00	12,300.00			
Year end 31/03/-5			3,075.00	9,225.00			
Year end 31/03/-6			0.00	0.00		8,000.00	14/02/-6
AB54 PZE	01/01/-5	15,200.00			Part-exchange		
Year end 31/03/-5			3,800.00	11,400.00			
Year end 31/03/-6			2,850.00	8,550.00			

Tutorial notes:

- installation of the pressing machine is capitalised

- the service contract is revenue expenditure

9.6 (d) Bank loan

(e) Hire purchase

10 Control accounts

10.1

Error	Difference	No difference
(a) Sales returns day book was undercast by £100	✔	
(b) A credit note for £75 was credited to the account of Martley Traders instead of Martley Manufacturing – both are sales ledger accounts		✔
(c) The sales ledger account of C Fernandez, £125, has been written off as irrecoverable, but no entry has been made in sales ledger control account	✔	
(d) A set-off entry for £45 has been incorrectly recorded as £54 in the sales ledger control account and in the sales ledger account		✔

10.2

		£
Total of list of purchases ledger balances		55,946
Adjustment for (a)	add	18
Adjustment for (b)	subtract	200
Adjustment for (c)	subtract	141
Adjustment for (d)	subtract	225
Revised total to agree with purchases ledger control account		55,398

10.3

Dr			VAT Control Account			Cr
20-1		£	20-1			£
31 Jan	Purchases	11,046	1 Jan	Balance b/d		6,240
31 Jan	Sales returns	722	31 Jan	Purchases returns		498
31 Jan	Non-current assets	1,845	31 Jan	Cash sales		864
31 Jan	Bank	6,240	31 Jan	Credit sales		18,347
31 Jan	Balance c/d	6,096				
		25,949				25,949
			1 Feb	Balance b/d		6,096

10.4

Dr			Payroll Control Account		Cr
20-2		£	20-2		£
28 Feb	Bank	11,367	28 Feb	Wages expenses	17,342
28 Feb	Pension fund	2,025			
28 Feb	Trade union fees	295			
28 Feb	HM Revenue & Customs	3,655			
		17,342			17,342

10.5

Adjustment number	Debit £	Credit £
1		120
3		100
4		95

10.6

Adjustment number	Debit £	Credit £
1		500
2	190	
4	280	

10.7

Adjustment number	Debit £	Credit £
2		360
3		90
4		120

11 The journal and correction of errors

11.1   (d)   Bank payment to a trade payable

11.2   (c)

Debit		Credit	
Stationery	£25	Office equipment	£25

11.3   (a)

Debit		Credit	
Suspense	£36	Vehicle repairs	£36
Vehicle repairs	£63	Suspense	£63

11.4

			Profit increases	Profit decreases
(a)	Sales account overcast			✔
(b)	Closing inventory undervalued		✔	
(c)	Telephone expenses account undercast			✔
(d)	Discounts received omitted		✔	
(e)	Depreciation charges for vehicles omitted			✔
(f)	Irrecoverable debt not written off			✔
(g)	Decrease in allowance for doubtful debts not made		✔	

11.5 **(a)** **Journal**

	Dr £	Cr £
Irrecoverable debts	300	
Sales ledger control		300

(b) **Journal**

	Dr £	Cr £
Office equipment	4,000	
Suspense		4,000

(c) **Journal**

	Dr £	Cr £
Closing inventory – statement of financial position	*18,140	
Closing inventory – statement of profit or loss		*18,140

* lower of cost and net realisable value: £18,380 – £240

(d) **Journal**

	Dr £	Cr £
VAT	920	
Suspense		920
VAT	920	
Suspense		920

11.6 Extended trial balance

Ledger account	Ledger balances		Adjustments		Statement of profit or loss		Statement of financial position	
	Dr £	Cr £	Dr £	Cr £	Dr £	Cr £	Dr £	Cr £
Allowance for doubtful debts		1,200	100					1,100
Allowance for doubtful debts adjustment				100		100		
Bank	15,300						15,300	
Capital		30,000						30,000
Closing inventory			25,230	25,230		25,230	25,230	
Depreciation charges			2,500		2,500			
Office equipment at cost	20,000						20,000	
Office equipment: accumulated depreciation		8,500		2,500				11,000
Office expenses	12,700		500		13,200			
Opening inventory	22,680				22,680			
Payroll expenses	25,920			350	25,570			
Purchases	85,500		400		85,900			
Purchases ledger control		25,270						25,270
Rent and rates	5,400			250	5,150			
Sales		151,200				151,200		
Sales ledger control	30,380						30,380	
Suspense	300		600	900				
VAT		2,010						2,010
Profit/loss for the year					21,530			21,530
	218,180	218,180	29,330	29,330	176,530	176,530	90,910	90,910

Tutorial note: the debit balance on suspense account is cleared by the debit adjustment of £600 (£350 and £250), and the credit adjustment of £900 (£500 and £400).

Practice
assessment 1

This Practice Assessment contains five tasks and you should attempt to complete every task.

Each task is independent. You will not need to refer to your answers to previous tasks.

Read every task carefully to make sure you understand what is required.

The standard rate of VAT is 20%.

Where the date is relevant, it is given in the task data.

Both minus signs and brackets can be used to indicate negative numbers unless task instructions say otherwise.

You must use a full stop to indicate a decimal point. For example, write 100.57 NOT 100,57 or 100 57

You may use a comma to indicate a number in the thousands, but you don't have to. For example 10000 and 10,000 are both acceptable.

Task 1

This task is about non-current assets. You are working for a business known as Toynton Trading. Toynton Trading is registered for VAT and has a financial year-end of 31 March.

The following is an extract from a purchase invoice received by Toynton Trading relating to a laptop computer to be used by the sales manager.

To: Toynton Trading Toynton House The High Road Toynton TN2 7RD	Invoice 2945 Laptop Supplies plc Unit 10, Fairway Estate Wyvern WV1 2XR		Date: 26 March 20-0
Item	**Details**	**Quantity**	**Total £**
PHX laptop computer	Serial no 415762XZ	1	740.00
Next-day delivery		1	10.00
Printer cartridge		1	20.00
VAT @ 20%			154.00
Total			924.00
Settlement terms: strictly 30 days net			

Toynton Trading paid the invoice in full on 10 April 20-0.

The following information relates to the sale of a car no longer required by the business:

Description	2.0 litre car PT07 PZV
Date of sale	14 March 20-0
Selling price	£7,500.00

- Toynton Trading has a policy of capitalising expenditure over £500.
- Vehicles are depreciated at 25% on a diminishing balance basis.
- Computer equipment is depreciated at 30% on a straight-line basis assuming no residual value.
- A full year's depreciation is applied in the year of acquisition and none in the year of disposal.

(a) Complete the extract from the non-current asset register on the next page for:
- Any acquisitions of non-current assets during the year ended 31 March 20-0.
- Any disposals of non-current assets during the year ended 31 March 20-0.
- Depreciation for the year ended 31 March 20-0 .

Notes:
- Not every cell will require an entry
- Show your answers to two decimal places
- Use the DD/MM/YY format for any dates

Extract from non-current assets register

Description/ serial no	Acquisition date	Cost £	Depreciation charges £	Carrying amount £	Funding method	Disposal proceeds £	Disposal date
Computer equipment							
PHX Laser printer	15/12/-7	1,200.00			Cash		
Year-end 31/03/-8			360.00	840.00			
Year-end 31/03/-9			360.00	480.00			
Year-end 31/03/-0							
Year-end 31/03/-0							
Vehicles							
PT07 PZV	20/05/-7	16,000.00			Hire purchase		
Year-end 31/03/-8			4,000.00	12,000.00			
Year-end 31/03/-9			3,000.00	9,000.00			
Year-end 31/03/-0							
PT58 ZPE	19/11/-8	14,400.00			Part-exchange		
Year-end 31/03/-9			3,600.00	10,800.00			
Year-end 31/03/-0							

(b) Complete the following sentence:

The financing method whereby ownership of an asset usually passes to the user at the end of the finance agreement is known as [   ].

Select from the following: cash purchase, finance lease, hire purchase, loan, part-exchange

Who is the appropriate person in a business to give authority for capital expenditure for a new machine for a workshop? Choose **one**.

(a)	The operator of the machine	
(b)	The owner of the business	
(c)	The firm's bank manager	
(d)	The workshop supervisor	

Task 2

This task is about ledger accounting for non-current assets.

- You are working on the accounting records of a business for the year ended 31 March 20-0.
- The business is registered for VAT.
- A new machine has been acquired. VAT can be reclaimed on this machine.
- The cost excluding VAT was £6,000; this was paid from the bank.
- The residual value is expected to be £2,000 excluding VAT.
- The depreciation policy for machines is that they are depreciated on a straight-line basis over five years. A full year's depreciation is applied in the year of acquisition.
- Depreciation has already been entered into the accounts for the existing machines.

(a)   Calculate the depreciation charges for the year on the new machine.

£ [   ] depreciation charge

Make entries to account for:

- The acquisition of the new machine
- The depreciation charge on the new machine

On each account, show clearly the balance carried down or transferred to the statement of profit or loss (profit or loss account) as appropriate.

Select your entries from the following list:

Balance b/d, Balance c/d, Bank, Depreciation charges, Disposals, Machinery accumulated depreciation, Machinery at cost, Profit or loss account, Purchases, Purchases ledger control, Sales, Sales ledger control.

Machinery at cost

Balance b/d	£25,000		

Machinery depreciation charges

Balance b/d	£1,000		

Machinery accumulated depreciation

		Balance b/d	£8,000

(b) The business keeps a non-current asset register of the machinery owned by the business. Which **one** of the following statements regarding a non-current asset register is **true**?

(a) It shows the carrying amount of each machine	
(b) It proves legal ownership of each machine	
(c) It shows how much each machine will be sold for when it is disposed	
(d) It shows when it is time to replace each machine	

(c) The business has sold a vehicle which originally cost £10,000. The proceeds of £4,000 were paid into the bank.

Which of the following entries for the proceeds is correct?

(a) Debit Disposals; credit Bank	
(b) Debit Vehicle at cost; credit Bank	
(c) Debit Bank; credit Disposals	
(d) Debit Bank; credit Vehicles at cost	

Task 3

This task is about ledger accounting, including accruals and prepayments, and applying ethical principles.

(a) Enter the figures given in the table below in the appropriate trial balance columns.

Do not enter zeros in unused columns. Do not enter any figures as negatives.

Extract from the trial balance as at 31 March 20-1	Ledger balance	Trial balance	
Account	£	Dr £	Cr £
Accrued income	584		
Discounts received	1,027		
Loan from bank	6,500		
Prepaid expenses	345		

You are working on the accounting records of a business for the year ended 31 March 20-1.

In this task, you can ignore VAT.

Business policy: accounting for accruals and prepayments

An entry is made into the income or expense account and an opposite entry into the relevant asset or liability account. In the following period, this entry is reversed.

You are looking at commission income for the year.

- The balance on the commission income account at the beginning of the financial year is £600. This represents an accrual for commission income as at the end of the year on 31 March 20-0.

- The cash book for the year shows receipts for commission income of £7,000.

- The commission income account has been correctly adjusted for £750 commission for the month of March 20-1. This was received into the bank and entered into the cash book on 7 April 20-1.

- Double-entry accounting is done in the general ledger.

(b) Complete the following statements by calculating the required figure and selecting **one** option from each box.

On 1 April 20-0, the commission income account shows a | DEBIT / CREDIT |
balance of £ [   ]

On 31 March 20-1, the commission income account shows an adjustment for

| ACCRUED EXPENSES |
| ACCRUED INCOME | of £ [   ]
| PREPAID EXPENSES |
| PREPAID INCOME |

(c)   Calculate the commission income for the year ended 31 March 20-1.

£ [ ]

You are now looking at selling expenses for the year.

- The cash book for the year shows payments for selling expenses of £6,420.

- The cash book payments for the year include £525 for website services for the three months ended 30 April 20-1. Website services are classified under selling expenses.

(d)   Update the selling expenses account. Show clearly:

- the cash book figure

- the year-end adjustment

- the transfer to the statement of profit or loss (profit or loss account) for the year

Select your entries from the following list:

Accrued expenses, Accrued income, Balance b/d, Balance c/d, Bank, Prepaid expenses, Prepaid income, Profit or loss account, Purchases, Purchases ledger control, Rent income, Sales, Sales ledger control, Selling expenses.

Selling expenses

	£		£
		Accrued expenses (reversal)	360

(e)   You are preparing the accounts of a business for the year to 31 March 20-1.

The owner of the business purchased a new delivery van and hands you the invoice for £12,000 dated 12 April 20-1. How will you treat this invoice in the accounts? Choose **one** answer for each row.

Invoice for delivery van dated 10 April 20-1	Acceptable treatment	Not acceptable treatment
The transaction is an expense relevant for the year to 31 March 20-2.		
The amount will be a non-current asset at 31 March 20-2 less depreciation charges.		
You record the transaction for the year to 31 March 20-1 in order to reduce the business profit for the year.		

Task 4

This task is about accounting adjustments.

You are a trainee accounting technician reporting to a managing partner in an accounting practice. You are working on the accounting records of a business client.

A trial balance (which follows) has been drawn up and balanced using a suspense account. You now need to make some corrections and adjustments for the year ended 31 March 20-5.

You may ignore VAT in this task.

The year's depreciation for machinery, at 20% diminishing balance, needs to be calculated and an adjustment made.

(a) Calculate the value of the depreciation charges adjustment.

£

(b) **(1)** Record the depreciation charges adjustment in the extract from the extended trial balance which follows.

(2) Make the following further adjustments.

You will NOT need to enter adjustments on every line.

Do NOT enter zeros into the unused cells.

- An irrecoverable debt of £150 is to be written off.

- A payment for rent of £600 has been made from the bank. The correct entry has been made to the bank account, but there was no corresponding entry.

- No entries have been made for closing inventory which has been valued at cost of £18,300. Included in this figure are some items that cost £2,020 but which will be sold for £1,500.

Extract from the extended trial balance

Ledger account	Ledger balances		Adjustments	
	Dr £	**Cr £**	**Dr £**	**Cr £**
Bank		10,345		
Capital		105,650		
Closing inventory				
Depreciation charges				
Irrecoverable debts	420			
Machinery at cost	52,500			
Machinery accumulated depreciation		10,500		
Opening inventory	6,225			
Purchases	70,110			
Purchases ledger control		10,340		
Rent paid	15,150			
Sales		132,305		
Sales ledger control	28,960			
VAT		12,380		
Suspense	600			

(c) Show the journal entries that will be required to close off the purchases account for the financial year-end.

Select your entries from the following list: Bank, Capital, Closing inventory, Depreciation charges, Irrecoverable debts, Machinery accumulated depreciation, Machinery at cost, Opening inventory, Profit or loss account, Purchases, Purchases ledger control account, Rent paid, Sales, Sales ledger control account, Statement of financial position, Suspense, VAT.

Journal

	Dr £	Cr £

Which of the following narratives is correct for the journal entries? Choose **one**.

(a)	Transfer of purchases for the year ended 31 March 20-5 to the profit or loss account	
(b)	Closure of purchases account to the purchases ledger control account	
(c)	Closure of general ledger for the year ended 31 March 20-5	
(d)	Transfer of purchases for the year ended 31 March 20-5 to the statement of financial position	

(d) Your manager has now reviewed the resulting figures in the draft accounts. She is concerned that the client may have significantly overstated the closing inventory figure, and this will need further investigation.

You know that the client needs to have the final accounts completed as quickly as possible ready for a meeting with the bank manager to arrange a business loan.

What should you and your manager do next, and why?

Choose **one**.

(a)	Complete the accounts quickly and without further adjustment, as any change is unlikely to be relevant to the meeting	
(b)	Arrange to carry out an investigation of the closing inventory and delay completion of the accounts, as any adjustment could affect the outcome of the meeting at the bank	
(c)	Reduce the value of the closing inventory by 50% so as to complete the accounts quickly, explaining to the client that this will reduce profit for the year and the tax that will be paid	
(d)	Arrange to carry out an investigation of the closing inventory and delay completion of the accounts, giving the client a copy of last year's accounts to show to the bank manager	

Task 5

This task is about period end routines, using accounting records, and the extended trial balance.

You are preparing the sales ledger control account for a sole trader.

The balance showing on sales ledger control account is a debit of £26,570 and the total of the account balances in the sales ledger is a debit of £26,230.

The sales ledger control account has been compared with sales ledger and the following points noted:

1   The total column of sales returns day book has been overcast (overadded) by £50.

2   £110 of discounts allowed has been entered in the sales ledger accounts but has been omitted from sales ledger control account.

3   A credit sale of £290 has been debited to the sales ledger account of Hart Ltd instead of the sales ledger account of Chart Ltd.

4   The account of Abbas Ltd, £280, has been written off as irrecoverable in sales ledger, but has not been recorded in sales ledger control account.

5   A set-off entry for £220 has been credited to the sales ledger account of Bilton Limited instead of to the sales ledger account of Bolton Limited.

6   A faster payments bank transfer sent by a credit customer was for £350, but the amount that should have been paid is £380.

(a)   Use the following table to show the **three** items that should appear in the sales ledger control account. Enter only **one** figure for each line. Do not enter zeros in unused cells.

Adjustment number	Debit £	Credit £

(b)   Which of the following statements about VAT control account is **true**? Choose **one**.

The VAT control account...

(a) ...has a debit balance when the business owes VAT to HM Revenue & Customs	
(b) ...records VAT on sales made by the business on the debit side	
(c) ...has a credit balance when a refund of VAT by HM Revenue & Customs is due to the business	
(d) ...records VAT on expenses of the business on the debit side	

(c)   You are now working on the accounting records of a different business.

You have the following extended trial balance. The adjustments have already been correctly entered.

Extend the figures into the statement of profit or loss and statement of financial position columns.

Do NOT enter zeros into unused column cells.

Complete the extended trial balance by entering figures and a label (*see below) in the correct places.

Extended trial balance

Ledger account	Ledger balances Dr £	Cr £	Adjustments Dr £	Cr £	Statement of profit or loss Dr £	Cr £	Statement of financial position Dr £	Cr £
Allowance for doubtful debts		2,100	250					
Allowance for doubtful debts adjustment				250				
Bank	3,700			200				
Capital		40,000						
Closing inventory			21,300	21,300				
Depreciation charges			2,750					
Machinery at cost	25,000							
Machinery accumulated depreciation		11,500		2,750				
Office expenses	7,350			300				
Opening inventory	19,100							
Payroll expenses	16,850		500					
Purchases	76,200							
Purchases ledger control		11,400						
Sales		118,200	450					
Sales ledger control	30,950							
Selling expenses	5,750							
Suspense	450		500	950				
VAT		2,150						
*								
TOTAL	185,350	185,350	25,750	25,750				

* Select your entry from the following list:

Balance b/d, Balance c/d, Gross profit/loss for the year, Profit/loss for the year, Suspense.

Practice
assessment 2

This Practice Assessment contains five tasks and you should attempt to complete every task.

Each task is independent. You will not need to refer to your answers to previous tasks.

Read every task carefully to make sure you understand what is required.

The standard rate of VAT is 20%.

Where the date is relevant, it is given in the task data.

Both minus signs and brackets can be used to indicate negative numbers unless task instructions say otherwise.

You must use a full stop to indicate a decimal point. For example, write 100.57 NOT 100,57 or 100 57

You may use a comma to indicate a number in the thousands, but you don't have to. For example 10000 and 10,000 are both acceptable.

Task 1

This task is about non-current assets. You are working for a business known as Selby Supplies. Selby Supplies is registered for VAT and has a financial year-end of 31 March.

The following is an extract from a purchase invoice received by Selby Supplies relating to a printer to be used in its office:

To: Selby Supplies Unit 4, Onslow Estate Onslow ON3 8PT	Invoice 3945 Office Supplies Ltd 80 Commercial Way Alminster AL2 1JK		Date: 20 February 20-0
Item	**Details**	**Quantity**	**Total £**
HQ Laser printer	Serial no HQ765943X	1	300.00
Next-day delivery		1	15.00
Toner cartridges		2	110.00
VAT @ 20%			85.00
Total			510.00
Settlement terms: strictly 30 days net			

Selby Supplies paid the invoice in full on 12 March 20-0.

The following information relates to the sale of a vehicle no longer required by the business:

Description	1.4 litre car AL57 AJH
Date of sale	20 March 20-0
Selling price	£4,000.00

- Selby Supplies has a policy of capitalising expenditure over £250.
- Vehicles are depreciated at 25% on a diminishing balance basis.
- Office equipment is depreciated at 20% on a straight-line basis assuming no residual value.
- A full year's depreciation is applied in the year of acquisition and none in the year of disposal.

(a) Complete the extract from the non-current assets register on the next page for:

- Any acquisitions of non-current assets during the year ended 31 March 20-0.
- Any disposals of non-current assets during the year ended 31 March 20-0.
- Depreciation for the year ended 31 March 20-0.

Notes:
- Not every cell will require an entry
- Show your answers to two decimal places
- Use the DD/MM/YY format for any dates

Extract from non-current assets register

Description/ serial no	Acquisition date	Cost £	Depreciation charges £	Carrying amount £	Funding method	Disposal proceeds £	Disposal date
Office equipment							
Astra desktop computer	19/01/-8	1,400.00			Cash		
Year-end 31/03/-8			280.00	1,120.00			
Year-end 31/03/-9			280.00	840.00			
Year-end 31/03/-0							
Year-end 31/03/-0							
Vehicles							
AL57 AJH	14/10/-7	12,800.00			Hire purchase		
Year-end 31/03/-8			3,200.00	9,600.00			
Year-end 31/03/-9			2,400.00	7,200.00			
Year-end 31/03/-0							
PT08 ZPE	17/06X8	15,200.00			Part-exchange		
Year-end 31/03/-9			3,800.00	11,400.00			
Year-end 31/03/-0							

(b)   Complete the following sentence:

The financing method whereby a business makes regular payments and has the use of an asset for a number of years, but ownership does not pass to the business is known as

[   ].

Select from the following: cash purchase, finance lease, hire purchase, loan, part-exchange

A business has bought a new machine and has incurred the following costs:

•	purchase price of the machine	£27,000
•	delivery costs of the machine	£500
•	cost of testing the machine	£1,000
•	cost of annual service contract	£750

Which cost should the business record as capital expenditure? Choose **one** answer.

(a)	£27,000	
(b)	£27,500	
(c)	£28,500	
(d)	£29,250	

Task 2

This task is about ledger accounting for non-current assets.

- You are working on the accounting records of a business for the year ended 31 March 20-2.
- The business is registered for VAT.
- A new vehicle has been acquired during the year. VAT can be reclaimed on this vehicle.
- The cost excluding VAT was £15,000; this was paid from the bank.
- The residual value is expected to be £5,000 excluding VAT.
- The depreciation policy for vehicles is that they are depreciated on a straight-line basis over four years. A full year's depreciation is applied in the year of acquisition.
- Depreciation has already been entered into the accounts for the existing vehicles.

(a) Calculate the depreciation charges for the year on the new vehicle.

£ [   ] depreciation charge

Make entries to account for:

- The acquisition of the new vehicle
- The depreciation charge on the new vehicle

On each account, show clearly the balance carried down or transferred to the statement of profit or loss (profit or loss account) as appropriate.

Select your entries from the following list:

Balance b/d, Balance c/d, Bank, Disposals, Profit or loss account, Purchases, Purchases ledger control, Sales ledger control, Vehicles accumulated depreciation, Vehicles at cost, Vehicle depreciation charges.

Vehicles at cost

Balance b/d	£95,000		

Vehicles depreciation charges

Balance b/d	£9,000		

Vehicles accumulated depreciation

		Balance b/d	£32,000

(b) The owner of the business is concerned that the carrying amount of one of the vehicles is lower than its market value. The owner asks if the depreciation rate for this vehicle should be changed to correct this.

Choose the **one** reply you will give to the owner.

(a)	No, because after they have been chosen, depreciation rates cannot be changed	
(b)	Yes, because a reduced rate of depreciation will increase the bank balance	
(c)	No, because the purpose of depreciation is to spread the cost of the asset over its useful life	
(d)	Yes, because the purpose of depreciation is to reflect the market value of the asset	

(c) The business has sold an item of office equipment which originally cost £2,000. The proceeds of £500 were paid into the bank.

Show the journal entries required to remove the original cost of the office equipment from the general ledger.

Account	Debit £	Credit £

Select your account names from the following list:

Bank, Depreciation charges, Disposals, Office equipment accumulated depreciation, Office equipment at cost, Profit or loss account, Purchases, Purchases ledger control, Sales, Sales ledger control, Suspense, Vehicles accumulated depreciation, Vehicles at cost.

Task 3

This task is about ledger accounting, including accruals and prepayments, and applying ethical principles.

(a)   Enter the figures given in the table below in the appropriate trial balance columns.

Do not enter zeros in unused columns. Do not enter any figures as negatives.

Extract from the trial balance as at 31 March 20-6	Ledger balance	Trial balance	
Account	£	**Dr £**	**Cr £**
Accrued expenses	362		
Carriage out	858		
Sales returns	1,246		
Prepaid income	126		

You are working on the accounting records of a business for the year ended 31 March 20-6.

In this task, you can ignore VAT.

Business policy: accounting for accruals and prepayments
An entry is made into the income or expense account and an opposite entry into the relevant asset or liability account. In the following period, this entry is reversed.

You are looking at rent paid for the year.

- The balance on the rent payable account at the beginning of the financial year is £750. This represents a prepayment for rent paid as at the end of the year on 31 March 20-5.

- The cash book for the year shows payments for rent of £8,650.

- The rent paid account has been correctly adjusted for £3,000 rent for the quarter ended 31 May 20-6. This was paid from the bank and entered into the cash book on 27 March 20-6.

- Double-entry accounting is done in the general ledger.

(b)   Calculate the value of the adjustment required for rent paid as at 31 March 20-6.

£ _____

Update the rent paid account. Show clearly:

- the cash book figure
- the year-end adjustment
- the transfer to the statement of profit or loss (profit or loss account) for the year

Select your entries from the following list:

Accrued expenses, Accrued income, Balance b/d, Balance c/d, Bank, Commission income, Prepaid expenses, Prepaid income, Profit or loss account, Purchases, Purchases ledger control, Rent paid, Sales, Sales ledger control, Statement of financial position.

Rent paid

	£		£
Prepaid expenses (reversal)	750		

You are now looking at commission income for the year.

Commission income of £270 was prepaid on 31 March 20-5.

(c)   Complete the following statements:

31 March 20-5
1 April 20-5
31 March 20-6
1 April 20-6

The reversal of the prepayment is dated

The reversal is on the | debit / credit | side of the commission income account.

·   The cash book for the year shows receipts for commission income of £2,425.

·   Commission of £360 for the two months ended 30 April 20-6 was received into the bank on 2 May 20-6.

(d)   Taking into account all the information you have, calculate the commission income for the year ended 31 March 20-6.

£ [   ]

(e)   Your junior colleague asks you to explain the accounting treatment of the commission income received on 2 May.

Which of the following can you use in your explanation to her? Choose **one** answer for each row.

Treatment of receipt dated 2 May	Acceptable treatment	Not acceptable treatment
The whole amount is treated as an expense for the financial year in which it is received		
The amount is apportioned pro-rata between the financial years ended 31 March 20-6 and 20-7		
The whole amount is treated as an expense for the period ended 31 March 20-6		

Task 4

This task is about accounting adjustments.

You are a trainee accounting technician reporting to a managing partner in an accounting practice. You are working on the accounting records of a business client.

A trial balance (which follows) has been drawn up and balanced using a suspense account. You now need to make some corrections and adjustments for the year ended 31 March 20-4.

You may ignore VAT in this task.

The allowance for doubtful debts needs to be adjusted to 2% of the outstanding trade receivables.

(a)   Calculate the value of the allowance for doubtful debts adjustment.

£

(b)   **(1)**   Record the allowance for doubtful debts adjustment in the extract from the extended trial balance which follows.

(2)   Make the following further adjustments.

You will NOT need to enter adjustments on every line.

Do NOT enter zeros into the unused cells.

- Sales of £1,220 have been posted to rent income account in error.

- The year's depreciation for machinery, at 25% diminishing balance, needs to be calculated and an adjustment made.

- A payment for office expenses of £225 has been posted correctly to bank account but has been posted to the wrong side of office expenses account.

Extract from the extended trial balance

Ledger account	Ledger balances		Adjustments	
	Dr £	Cr £	Dr £	Cr £
Allowance for doubtful debts		365		
Allowance for doubtful debts – adjustment				
Bank		10,320		
Depreciation charges				
Irrecoverable debts	210			
Machinery at cost	50,000			
Machinery accumulated depreciation		12,500		
Office expenses	5,295			
Purchases	56,105			
Purchases ledger control		9,360		
Rent income		18,140		
Sales		102,310		
Sales ledger control	16,550			
VAT		2,045		
Suspense	450			

(c) Show the journal entries that will be required to close off the purchases account for the financial year-end.

Select your entries from the following list: Allowance for doubtful debts, Allowance for doubtful debts – adjustment, Bank, Depreciation charges, Irrecoverable debts, Machinery accumulated depreciation, Machinery at cost, Office expenses, Profit or loss account, Purchases, Purchases ledger control account, Rent income, Sales, Sales ledger control account, Statement of financial position, Suspense, VAT.

Journal

	Dr £	Cr £

Which of the following narratives is correct for the journal entries? Choose **one**.

(a)	Closure of general ledger for the year ended 31 March 20-4	
(b)	Closure of irrecoverable debts account to the purchases ledger control account	
(c)	Transfer of irrecoverable debts for the year ended 31 March 20-4 to the statement of financial position	
(d)	Transfer of irrecoverable debts for the year ended 31 March 20-4 to the profit or loss account	

(d) Your manager has now reviewed the resulting figures in the draft accounts. She is concerned that the client may have significantly understated depreciation charges, and this will need further investigation.

You know that the client needs to have the final accounts completed ready for a meeting with the bank manager to arrange an increase in the overdraft limit.

What should you and your manager do next, and why?

Choose **one**.

(a)	Complete the accounts without further adjustment, advising the client to tell the bank manager that depreciation charges do not affect the bank balance	
(b)	Before completing the accounts, arrange a meeting with the client to review the depreciation policies of the business	
(c)	Complete the accounts quickly, without further adjustment, as you know that the client wishes to take the profit for the year from the bank account as personal drawings before meeting with the bank manager	
(d)	Increase the depreciation charges by 50%, without reference to the client, so as to complete the accounts quickly	

Task 5

This task is about period end routines, using accounting records, and the extended trial balance.

You are preparing the purchases ledger control account for a sole trader.

The balance showing on purchases ledger control account is a credit of £33,943 and the total of the account balances in purchases ledger is a credit of £33,860.

The purchases ledger has been compared with purchases ledger control account and the following points noted:

1   The total column of purchases returns day book has been overcast (overadded) by £100.

2   A credit purchase of £750 from Bristan Ltd has been credited to the purchases ledger account of Tristan Ltd.

3   A payment of £284 has been debited to the purchases ledger account of Mark Andrews instead of the purchases ledger account of Andrew Marks.

4   A BACS payment sent to a credit supplier was for £290, but the amount that should have been paid is £320.

5   A set-off entry for £125 has been recorded in purchases ledger control account as £152.

6   £105 of discounts received from trade payables has been entered on the wrong side of purchases ledger control account.

(a)   Use the following table to show the **three** items that should appear in the purchases ledger control account. Enter only **one** figure for each line. Do not enter zeros in unused cells.

Adjustment number	Debit £	Credit £

(b)   Which of the following statements about payroll control account is **true**? Choose **one**.

The payroll control account...

(a) ...shows separate entries for each employee	
(b) ...has a debit balance when all entries have been correctly made	
(c) ...records the totals from all of the payroll transactions carried out each time the payroll is run	
(d) ...is another name for wages expense account	

(c)   You are now working on the accounting records of a different business.

This task is about the extended trial balance and showing your knowledge of good accounting practice.

You have the following extended trial balance. The adjustments have already been correctly entered.

Extend the figures into the statement of profit or loss and statement of financial position columns.

Do NOT enter zeros into unused column cells.

Complete the extended trial balance by entering figures and a label (see * below) in the correct places.

Extended trial balance

Ledger account	Ledger balances		Adjustments		Statement of profit or loss		Statement of financial position	
	Dr £	**Cr £**	**Dr £**	**Cr £**	**Dr £**	**Cr £**	**Dr £**	**Cr £**
Allowance for doubtful debts		790		120				
Allowance for doubtful debts adjustment			120					
Bank		3,200	150					
Capital		25,000						
Closing inventory			16,920	16,920				
Depreciation charges			3,150					
Irrecoverable debts	225							
Office equipment at cost	17,350							
Office equipment accumulated depreciation		5,170		3,150				
Office expenses	16,840			370				
Opening inventory	12,960							
Purchases	62,040		180					
Purchases ledger control		8,450						
Sales		109,245						
Sales ledger control	25,160							
Selling expenses	20,210			580				
Suspense		620	950	330				
Value Added Tax		2,310						
*								
TOTAL	154,785	154,785	21,470	21,470				

* Select your entry from the following list:

Balance b/d, Balance c/d, Gross profit/loss for the year, Profit/loss for the year, Suspense.

Practice
assessment 3

This Practice Assessment contains five tasks and you should attempt to complete every task.

Each task is independent. You will not need to refer to your answers to previous tasks.

Read every task carefully to make sure you understand what is required.

The standard rate of VAT is 20%.

Where the date is relevant, it is given in the task data.

Both minus signs and brackets can be used to indicate negative numbers unless task instructions say otherwise.

You must use a full stop to indicate a decimal point. For example, write 100.57 NOT 100,57 or 100 57

You may use a comma to indicate a number in the thousands, but you don't have to. For example 10000 and 10,000 are both acceptable.

Task 1

This task is about non-current assets. You are working for a business known as Tyler Trading. Tyler Trading is registered for VAT and has a financial year-end of 31 March.

The following is an extract from a purchase invoice received by Tyler Trading relating to some items to be used in its office:

To: Tyler Trading Tyler House 14 Blenheim Road Linton LT4 6AR	Invoice 7341 Copier Services Ltd 28 Booth Lane Burdish BD3 8AP		Date: 25 Nov 20-5
Item	**Details**	**Quantity**	**Total £**
Multifunction copier	Model XPL417	1	650.00
Toner cartridge	XPL4 Blk/Col	2	90.00
Installation		1	50.00
First year service contract		1	60.00
Total			850.00
Delivery date: 25/11/20-5			

Tyler Trading paid £850.00 to Copier Services Ltd on 28 November 20-5 with £850.00 borrowed interest-free from a third party. This amount is to be repaid in full on 31 December 20-7.

The following information relates to the sale of a delivery van no longer required by the business:

Description	2.0 litre van VU13 ZUP
Date of sale	10 March 20-6
Selling price	£4,000.00

- VAT can be ignored.
- Tyler Trading has a policy of capitalising expenditure over £500.
- Office equipment is depreciated at 30% per year on a straight-line basis.
- Vehicles are depreciated at 25% on a diminishing balance basis.
- A full year's depreciation is applied in the year of acquisition and none in the year of disposal.

(a) Complete the extract from the non-current assets register on the next page for:
- Any acquisitions of non-current assets during the year ended 31 March 20-6.
- Any disposals of non-current assets during the year ended 31 March 20-6.
- Depreciation for the year ended 31 March 20-6.

Notes:
- Not every cell will require an entry
- Show your answers to two decimal places
- Use the DD/MM/YY format for any dates

Extract from non-current assets register

Description/ serial no	Acquisition date	Cost £	Depreciation charges £	Carrying amount £	Funding method	Disposal proceeds £	Disposal date
Office equipment							
Laptop computer PT4	16/06/-4	750.00			Cash		
Year-end 31/03/-5			225.00	525.00			
Year-end 31/03/-6							
Year-end 31/03/-6							
Vehicles							
1.6 litre car VX63 PSX	20/09/-3	10,240.00			Hire purchase		
Year-end 31/03/-4			2,560.00	7,680.00			
Year-end 31/03/-5			1,920.00	5,760.00			
Year-end 31/03/-6							
2.0 litre van VU13 ZUP	02/04/-3	9,600.00			Cash		
Year-end 31/03/-4			2,400.00	7,200.00			
Year-end 31/03/-5			1,800.00	5,400.00			
Year-end 31/03/-6							

(b)   Complete the following sentence:

When a business trades in an old asset as either a partial payment or a deposit for a finance agreement it is referred to as [_____].

Select from the following: cash purchase, finance lease, hire purchase, loan, part-exchange

It is important to obtain authority from the appropriate person for capital expenditure in order to [_____].

Select from the following:

- ensure that the expenditure fits in with the business's plans and budgets
- comply with the requirements of IAS 16, *Property, plant and equipment*
- demonstrate that the business has applied the appropriate level of materiality

Task 2

This task is about ledger accounting for non-current assets.

You are working on the accounting records of a business for the year ended 31 March 20-6.

- VAT can be ignored.

- A machine was part-exchanged on 20 September 20-5.

- The original machine was bought for £6,700 on 10 August 20-1.

- Depreciation is provided at 15% per year on a straight-line basis.

- A full year's depreciation is applied in the year of acquisition and none in the year of disposal.

- A part-exchange allowance of £3,000 was given.

- £6,400 was paid from the bank to complete the purchase of the new machine.

(a) Make entries relating to the disposal:

- complete the disposals account

- update the bank account

On each account, show clearly the balance carried down or transferred to the statement of profit or loss (profit or loss account) as appropriate.

Select your entries from the following list:

Balance b/d, Balance c/d, Bank, Depreciation charges, Disposals, Machinery accumulated depreciation, Machinery at cost, Profit or loss account, Purchases, Purchases ledger control, Repair and maintenance costs, Sales, Sales ledger control.

Disposals

	£		£

Bank

	£		£
Balance b/d	15,365		

(b)   Calculate the total cost of the new machine.

£ [ ]

What will be the carrying amount of the new machine as at 31 March 20-7?

£ [ ]

(c)   A business has re-equipped its computer room and has incurred the following costs:

- purchase price of computers   £20,000
- installation of computers   £1,000
- testing of computers   £1,500
- insurance of computers   £750

What costs should the business record as capital expenditure and revenue expenditure? Choose **one** answer for each type of expenditure.

Capital expenditure	
£20,000	
£21,000	
£22,500	
£23,250	

Revenue expenditure	
£750	
£1,000	
£1,500	
£2,250	

Task 3

This task is about ledger accounting, including accruals and prepayments, and applying ethical principles.

(a) Enter the figures given in the table below in the appropriate trial balance columns.

Do not enter zeros in unused columns. Do not enter any figures as negatives.

Extract from the trial balance as at 31 March 20-6	Ledger balance	Trial balance	
Account	£	Dr £	Cr £
Accrued income	155		
Discounts received	546		
Purchases returns	1,048		
Prepaid expenses	392		

You are working on the accounting records of a business for the year ended 31 March 20-6.

In this task, you can ignore VAT.

Business policy: accounting for accruals and prepayments

An entry is made into the income or expense account and an opposite entry into the relevant asset or liability account. In the following period, this entry is reversed.

You are looking at rent income for the year.

- The balance on the rent income account at the beginning of the financial year is £2,400. This represents a prepayment for rent income as at the end of the year on 31 March 20-5.

- The cash book for the year shows receipts for rent income of £15,900.

- The rent income account has been correctly adjusted for £3,000 rent for the quarter ended 31 May 20-6. This was received into the bank and entered into the cash book on 28 March 20-6.

- Double-entry accounting is done in the general ledger.

(b) Complete the following statements by calculating the required figure and selecting **one** option from each box.

On 1 April 20-5, the rent income account shows a DEBIT / CREDIT

balance of £ [   ]

On 31 March 20-6, the rent income account shows an adjustment for

ACCRUED EXPENSES
ACCRUED INCOME
PREPAID EXPENSES
PREPAID INCOME

of £ [   ]

(c)   Calculate the rent income for the year ended 31 March 20-6.

£ [   ]

You are now looking at the electricity expenses for the year.

·   The cash book for the year shows payments for electricity expenses of £6,475.

·   There is a bill of £630 for electricity for the three months ended 30 April 20-6 that has not been included in the accounting records.

(d)   Update the electricity expenses account. Show clearly:

·   the cash book figure

·   the year-end adjustment

·   the transfer to the statement of profit or loss (profit or loss account) for the year

Select your entries from the following list:

Accrued expenses, Accrued income, Balance b/d, Balance c/d, Bank, Electricity expenses, Prepaid expenses, Prepaid income, Profit or loss account, Purchases, Purchases ledger control, Rent income, Sales, Sales ledger control.

Electricity expenses

	£		£
Prepaid expenses (reversal)	135		

(e)   You are now working on the accounting records of another business for the year to 31 March 20-6.

You have discovered that an expense for £3,000 for the year to 31 March 20-6 was paid on 20 April 20-6. This expense has not been included in the accounting records to 31 March 20-6. How will you treat this expense in the accounts? Choose **one** answer for each row.

Expense for £3,000 paid on 20 April 20-6	Acceptable treatment	Not acceptable treatment
The transaction is an expense relevant for the year to 31 March 20-7.		
The owner of the business asks you to record the transaction for the year to 31 March 20-7 in order to maximise profits for the year to 31 March 20-6.		
The transaction is an accrual for the year to 31 March 20-6 and will increase the expenses for that year.		

Task 4

This task is about accounting adjustments.

You are a trainee accounting technician reporting to a managing partner in an accounting practice. You are working on the accounting records of a business client.

A trial balance (which follows) has been drawn up and balanced using a suspense account. You now need to make some corrections and adjustments for the year ended 31 March 20-6.

You may ignore VAT in this task.

The year's depreciation for vehicles, at 25% diminishing balance, needs to be calculated and an adjustment made.

(a) Calculate the value of the depreciation charges adjustment.

£

(b) **(1)** Record the depreciation charges adjustment in the extract from the extended trial balance which follows.

(2) Make the following further adjustments.

You will NOT need to enter adjustments on every line.

Do NOT enter zeros into the unused cells.

- An irrecoverable debt of £200 is to be written off.

- The allowance for doubtful debts needs to be adjusted to £350.

- A receipt for rent income of £950 has been made into the bank. The correct entry has been made to the bank account, but there was no corresponding entry.

Extract from the extended trial balance

Ledger account	Ledger balances		Adjustments	
	Dr £	Cr £	Dr £	Cr £
Allowance for doubtful debts		375		
Allowance for doubtful debts – adjustment				
Bank		3,045		
Depreciation charges				
Irrecoverable debts	120			
Office expenses	16,225			
Purchases	65,045			
Purchases ledger control		12,390		
Rent income		12,040		
Sales		144,620		
Sales ledger control	38,345			
VAT		3,065		
Vehicles at cost	64,000			
Vehicles accumulated depreciation		16,000		
Suspense		950		

(c) Show the journal entries that will be required to close off the office expenses account for the financial year end.

Select your entries from the following list: Allowance for doubtful debts, Allowance for doubtful debts – adjustment, Bank, Depreciation charges, Irrecoverable debts, Office expenses, Profit or loss account, Purchases, Purchases ledger control account, Rent income, Sales, Sales ledger control account, Statement of financial position, Suspense, VAT, Vehicles accumulated depreciation, Vehicles at cost.

Journal

	Dr £	Cr £

Which of the following narratives is correct for the journal entries? Choose **one**.

(a)	Closure of general ledger for the year ended 31 March 20-6	
(b)	Closure of office expenses account to the VAT account	
(c)	Transfer of office expenses for the year ended 31 March 20-6 to the profit or loss account	
(d)	Transfer of office expenses for the year ended 31 March 20-6 to the statement of financial position	

(d) You work as a bookkeeper and are currently studying the AAT's Advanced Diploma in Accounting. A friend of yours owns a van and is self-employed as a removal business. Your friend asks you to prepare and sign off the business' year-end financial statements, insisting that the lowest possible profit is shown.

Indicate the ethical principle that is at issue.

(a)	Integrity	
(b)	Objectivity	
(c)	Professional competence and due care	
(d)	Confidentiality	
(e)	Professional behaviour	

Task 5

This task is about period end routines, using accounting records, and the extended trial balance.

You are preparing the bank reconciliation for a sole trader.

The balance showing on the bank statement is a debit of £1,550 and the balance in the cash book is a credit of £1,890.

The bank statement has been compared with the cash book and the following points noted:

1   A direct debit payment made by the bank for £540 has been incorrectly entered in the cash book as £450.

2   A bank lodgement for £1,135 made yesterday is not showing on the bank statement.

3   Receipts from cash sales of £360 have been entered in the cash book but are not yet banked.

4   There are unpresented cheques totalling £1,340.

5   Bank charges of £95 have not been entered in the cash book.

6   A faster payment receipt from a customer for £680 has not been entered in the cash book.

(a)   Use the following table to show the **three** items that should appear on the cash book side of the reconciliation. Enter only **one** figure for each line. Do not enter zeros in unused cells.

Adjustment number	Debit £	Credit £

(b)   Which of the following statements about sales ledger control account is **true**? Choose **one**.

The sales ledger control account...

(a)	...records the balances of sales account and sales returns account	
(b)	...does not record transactions to write off an irrecoverable debt	
(c)	...contains an account for each trade receivable and records the transactions with that customer	
(d)	...records the totals of all transactions passing through the sales ledger	

(c) You are now working on the accounting records of a different business.

You have the following extended trial balance. The adjustments have already been correctly entered.

Extend the figures into the statement of profit or loss and statement of financial position columns.

Do NOT enter zeros into unused column cells.

Complete the extended trial balance by entering figures and a label (see *below) in the correct places.

Extended trial balance

Ledger account	Ledger balances		Adjustments		Statement of profit or loss		Statement of financial position	
	Dr £	Cr £	Dr £	Cr £	Dr £	Cr £	Dr £	Cr £
Accruals				230				
Bank	9,420		85					
Capital		35,000		10,500				
Closing inventory			9,450	9,450				
Depreciation charges	4,700							
Drawings			10,500					
General expenses	26,081			346				
Machinery at cost	23,500							
Machinery accumulated depreciation		7,920						
Opening inventory	8,190							
Prepayments			346					
Purchases	58,484							
Purchases ledger control		7,368		247				
Rent receivable		2,765						
Sales		117,622						
Sales ledger control	13,378							
Suspense		162	247	85				
Wages	27,084		230					
*								
TOTAL								

* Select your entry from the following list:

Balance b/d, Balance c/d, Gross profit/loss for the year, Profit/loss for the year, Suspense.

Answers to practice assessment 1

Task 1 (a)

Extract from non-current assets register

Description/ serial no	Acquisition date	Cost £	Depreciation charges £	Carrying amount £	Funding method	Disposal proceeds £	Disposal date
Computer equipment							
PHX Laser printer	15/12/-7	1,200.00			Cash		
Year-end 31/03/-8			360.00	840.00			
Year-end 31/03/-9			360.00	480.00			
Year-end 31/03/-0			360.00	120.00			
PHX Laptop computer	26/03/-0	750.00			Cash		
Year-end 31/03/X0			225.00	525.00			
Vehicles							
PT07 PZV	20/05/-7	16,000.00			Hire purchase		
Year-end 31/03/X8			4,000.00	12,000.00			
Year-end 31/03/X9			3,000.00	9,000.00			
Year-end 31/03/X0			0.00	0.00		7,500.00	14/03/X0
PT58 ZPE	19/11/-8	14,400.00			Part-exchange		
Year-end 31/03/X9			3,600.00	10,800.00			
Year-end 31/03/X0			2,700.00	8,100.00			

Tutorial note: the delivery cost of the laptop computer is capitalised.

(b)   hire purchase

    (b)   The owner of the business

Task 2

(a) £800 depreciation charge

Machinery at cost

Balance b/d	£25,000	Balance c/d	£31,000
Bank	£6,000		
	£31,000		£31,000

Machinery depreciation charges

Balance b/d	£1,000	Profit or loss account	£1,800
Machinery accumulated depreciation	£800		
	£1,800		£1,800

Machinery accumulated depreciation

		Balance b/d	£8,000
Balance c/d	£8,800	Depreciation charges	£800
	£8,800		£8,800

(b) (a) It shows the carrying amount of each machine

(c) (c) Debit Bank; credit Disposals

Task 3

(a)

Extract from the trial balance as at 31 March 20-1	Ledger balance	Trial balance	
Account	£	Dr £	Cr £
Accrued income	584	584	
Discounts received	1,027		1,027
Loan from bank	6,500		6,500
Prepaid expenses	345	345	

(b) A DEBIT balance of £600.

An adjustment for ACCRUED INCOME of £750.

(c) £7,150, ie £7,000 – £600 + £750.

(d) **Selling expenses**

	£		£
Bank	6,420	Accrued expenses (reversal)	360
		Profit or loss account	5,885
		Prepaid expenses	175
	6,420		6,420

(e)

Invoice for delivery van dated 10 April 20-1	Acceptable treatment	Not acceptable treatment
The transaction is an expense relevant for the year to 31 March 20-2.		✔
The amount will be a non-current asset at 31 March 20-2 less depreciation charges.	✔	
You record the transaction for the year to 31 March 20-1 in order to reduce the business profit for the year.		✔

Task 4

(a)   £8,400

(b)   **Extract from the extended trial balance**

Ledger account	Ledger balances		Adjustments	
	Dr £	Cr £	Dr £	Cr £
Bank		10,345		
Capital		105,650		
Closing inventory			17,780	17,780
Depreciation charges			8,400	
Irrecoverable debts	420		150	
Machinery at cost	52,500			
Machinery accumulated depreciation		10,500		8,400
Opening inventory	6,225			
Purchases	70,110			
Purchases ledger control		10,340		
Rent paid	15,150			600
Sales		132,305		
Sales ledger control	28,960			150
VAT		12,380		
Suspense	600			600

(c) **Journal**

	Dr £	Cr £
Profit or loss account	70,110	
Purchases		70,110

(a) Transfer of purchases for the year ended 31 March 20-5 to the profit or loss account

(d) (b) Arrange to carry out an investigation of the closing inventory and delay completion of the accounts, as any adjustment could affect the outcome of the meeting at the bank.

Task 5

(a)

Adjustment number	Debit £	Credit £
1	50	
2		110
4		280

(b) (d) ...records VAT on expenses of the business on the debit side

(c)   Extended trial balance

Ledger account	Ledger balances		Adjustments		Statement of profit or loss		Statement of financial position	
	Dr £	Cr £	Dr £	Cr £	Dr £	Cr £	Dr £	Cr £
Allowance for doubtful debts		2,100	250					1,850
Allowance for doubtful debts adjustment				250		250		
Bank	3,700			200			3,500	
Capital		40,000						40,000
Closing inventory			21,300	21,300		21,300	21,300	
Depreciation charges			2,750		2,750			
Machinery at cost	25,000						25,000	
Machinery accumulated depreciation		11,500		2,750				14,250
Office expenses	7,350			300	7,050			
Opening inventory	19,100				19,100			
Payroll expenses	16,850		500		17,350			
Purchases	76,200				76,200			
Purchases ledger control		11,400						11,400
Sales		118,200	450			117,750		
Sales ledger control	30,950						30,950	
Selling expenses	5,750				5,750			
Suspense	450		500	950				
VAT		2,150						2,150
Profit/loss for the year					11,100			11,100
TOTAL	185,350	185,350	25,750	25,750	139,300	139,300	80,750	80,750

Tutorial note: the debit balance of £450 on suspense account is cleared by the debit adjustment for £500 (£200 and £300), and the credit adjustment for £950 (£500 and £450).

Answers to practice assessment 2

Task 1 (a)

Extract from non-current assets register

Description/ serial no	Acquisition date	Cost £	Depreciation charges £	Carrying amount £	Funding method	Disposal proceeds £	Disposal date
Office equipment							
Astra desktop computer	19/01/-8	1,400.00			Cash		
Year-end 31/03/-8			280.00	1,120.00			
Year-end 31/03/-9			280.00	840.00			
Year-end 31/03/-0			280.00	560.00			
HQ Laser printer	20/02/-0	315.00			Cash		
Year-end 31/03/-0			63.00	252.00			
Vehicles							
AL57 AJH	14/10/-7	12,800.00			Hire purchase		
Year-end 31/03/-8			3,200.00	9,600.00			
Year-end 31/03/-9			2,400.00	7,200.00			
Year-end 31/03/-0			0.00	0.00		4,000.00	20/03/-0
PT08 ZPE	17/06X8	15,200.00			Part-exchange		
Year-end 31/03/-9			3,800.00	11,400.00			
Year-end 31/03/-0			2,850.00	8,550.00			

(b)   finance lease

   (c)   £28,500

Task 2

(a)   £2,500 depreciation charge

Vehicles at cost

Balance b/d	£95,000	Balance c/d	£110,000
Bank	£15,000		
	£110,000		£110,000

Vehicles depreciation charges

Balance b/d	£9,000	Profit or loss account	£11,500
Vehicles accumulated dep'n	£2,500		
	£11,500		£11,500

Vehicles accumulated depreciation

Balance c/d	£34,500	Balance b/d	£32,000
		Depreciation charges	£2,500
	£34,500		£34,500

(b)   (c) No, because the purpose of depreciation is to spread the cost of the asset over its useful life.

(c)

Account	Debit £	Credit £
Disposals	2,000	
Office equipment at cost		2,000

Task 3

(a)

Extract from the trial balance as at 31 March 20-6	Ledger balance	Trial balance	
Account	£	Dr £	Cr £
Accrued expenses	362		362
Carriage out	858	858	
Sales returns	1,246	1,246	
Prepaid income	126		126

(b) Adjustment required for rent paid as at 31 March 20-6: £2,000

Rent of £1,000 per month for April and May

Rent paid

	£		£
Prepaid expenses (reversal)	750	Profit or loss account	7,400
Bank	8,650	Prepaid expenses	2,000
	9,400		9,400

(c) The reversal of the prepayment is dated 1 April 20-5.

The reversal is on the **credit** side of the commission income account.

(d) £2,875.   *£270 + £2,425 + £180 (pro rata).*

(e)

Treatment of receipt dated 2 May	Acceptable treatment	Not acceptable treatment
The whole amount is treated as an expense for the financial year in which it is received		✔
The amount is apportioned pro-rata between the financial years ended 31 March 20-6 and 20-7	✔	
The whole amount is treated as an expense for the period ended 31 March 20-6		✔

Task 4

(a)   –£34

(b)   **Extract from the extended trial balance**

Ledger account	Ledger balances		Adjustments	
	Dr £	**Cr** £	**Dr** £	**Cr** £
Allowance for doubtful debts		365	34	
Allowance for doubtful debts – adjustment				34
Bank		10,320		
Depreciation charges			9,375	
Irrecoverable debts	210			
Machinery at cost	50,000			
Machinery accumulated depreciation		12,500		9,375
Office expenses	5,295		450	
Purchases	56,105			
Purchases ledger control		9,360		
Rent income		18,140	1,220	
Sales		102,310		1,220
Sales ledger control	16,550			
VAT		2,045		
Suspense	450			450

(c)
Journal

	Dr £	**Cr** £
Profit or loss account	210	
Irrecoverable debts		210

(d)   Transfer of irrecoverable debts for the year ended 31 March 20-4 to the profit or loss account

(d)   (b)   Before completing the accounts, arrange a meeting with the client to review the depreciation policies of the business.

Task 5

(a)

Adjustment number	Debit £	Credit £
1		100
5		27
6	210	

(b)   **(c)** ...records the totals from all of the payroll transactions carried out each time the payroll is run

(c) **Extended trial balance**

Ledger account	Ledger balances		Adjustments		Statement of profit or loss		Statement of financial position	
	Dr £	Cr £	Dr £	Cr £	Dr £	Cr £	Dr £	Cr £
Allowance for doubtful debts		790		120				910
Allowance for doubtful debts adjustment			120			120		
Bank		3,200	150					3,050
Capital		25,000						25,000
Closing inventory			16,920	16,920		16,920	16,920	
Depreciation charge			3,150		3,150			
Irrecoverable debts	225				225			
Office equipment at cost	17,350						17,350	
Office equipment accumulated depreciation		5,170		3,150				8,320
Office expenses	16,840			370	16,470			
Opening inventory	12,960				12,960			
Purchases	62,040		180		62,220			
Purchases ledger control		8,450						8,450
Sales		109,245				109,245		
Sales ledger control	25,160						25,160	
Selling expenses	20,210			580	19,630			
Suspense		620	950	330				
Value Added Tax		2,310						2,310
Profit/loss for the year					11,390			11,390
TOTAL	154,785	154,785	21,470	21,470	126,165	126,165	59,430	59,430

Tutorial note: the credit balance of £620 on suspense account is cleared by the debit adjustment for £950 (£370 and £580), and the credit adjustment for £330 (£150 and £180)

Answers to practice assessment 3

Task 1 (a)

Extract from non-current assets register

Description/ serial no	Acquisition date	Cost £	Depreciation charges £	Carrying amount £	Funding method	Disposal proceeds £	Disposal date
Office equipment							
Laptop computer PT4	16/06/-4	750.00			Cash		
Year-end 31/03/-5			225.00	525.00			
Year-end 31/03/-6			225.00	300.00			
Copier XPL417	25/11/-5	700.00			Loan		
Year-end 31/03/-6			210.00	490.00			
Vehicles							
1.6 litre car VX63 PSX	20/09/-3	10,240.00			Hire purchase		
Year-end 31/03/-4			2,560.00	7,680.00			
Year-end 31/03/-5			1,920.00	5,760.00			
Year-end 31/03/-6			1,440.00	4,320.00			
2.0 litre van VU13 ZUP	02/04/-3	9,600.00			Cash		
Year-end 31/03/-4			2,400.00	7,200.00			
Year-end 31/03/-5			1,800.00	5,400.00			
Year-end 31/03/-6			0.00	0.00		4,000.00	10/03/-6

Tutorial note: the installation cost of the copier is capitalised.

(b)   part-exchange

ensure that the expenditure fits in with the business's plans and budgets

Task 2

(a)

Disposals

	£		£
Machinery at cost	6,700	Machinery accumulated depreciation	4,020
Profit or loss account	320	Machinery at cost	3,000
	7,020		7,020

Bank

	£		£
Balance b/d	15,365	Machinery at cost	6,400
		Balance c/d	8,965
	15,365		15,365

(b) £9,400 ie £3,000 + £6,400

£6,580 ie £9,400 − (£1,410 depreciation x 2 years)

(c) Capital expenditure   £22,500

Revenue expenditure   £750

Task 3

(a)

Extract from the trial balance as at 31 March 20-6	Ledger balance	Trial balance	
Account	£	Dr £	Cr £
Accrued income	155	155	
Discounts received	546		546
Purchases returns	1,048		1,048
Prepaid expenses	392	392	

(b) A CREDIT balance of £2,400.

An adjustment for PREPAID INCOME of £2,000.

(c) £16,300, ie £15,900 + £2,400 − £2,000.

(d) Electricity expenses

	£		£
Prepaid expenses reversal	135	Profit or loss account	7,030
Bank	6,475		
Accrued expenses	420		
	7,030		7,030

(e)

Expense for £3,000 paid on 20 April 20-6	Acceptable treatment	Not acceptable treatment
The transaction is an expense relevant for the year to 31 March 20-7.		✔
The owner of the bsuiness asks you to record the transaction for the year to 31 March 20-7 in order to maximise profits for the year to 31 March 20-6.		✔
The transaction is an accrual for the year to 31 March 20-6 and will increase the expenses for that year.	✔	

Task 4

(a)   £12,000

(b)   **Extract from the extended trial balance**

Ledger account	Ledger balances		Adjustments	
	Dr £	**Cr** £	**Dr** £	**Cr** £
Allowance for doubtful debts		375	25	
Allowance for doubtful debts – adjustment				25
Bank		3,045		
Depreciation charges			12,000	
Irrecoverable debts	120		200	
Office expenses	16,225			
Purchases	65,045			
Purchases ledger control		12,390		
Rent income		12,040		950
Sales		144,620		
Sales ledger control	38,345			200
VAT		3,065		
Vehicles at cost	64,000			
Vehicles accumulated depreciation		16,000		12,000
Suspense		950	950	

(c)
Journal

	Dr £	**Cr** £
Profit or loss account	16,225	
Office expenses		16,225

(c)   Transfer of office expenses for the year ended 31 March 20-6 to the profit or loss account

(d)   (e)   Professional behaviour

Task 5

(a)

Adjustment number	Debit £	Credit £
1		90
5		95
6	680	

(b)   (d) ...records the totals of all transactions passing through the sales ledger

(c)   Extended trial balance

Ledger account	Ledger balances		Adjustments		Statement of profit or loss		Statement of financial position	
	Dr £	Cr £	Dr £	Cr £	Dr £	Cr £	Dr £	Cr £
Accruals				230				230
Bank	9,420		85				9,505	
Capital		35,000		10,500				45,500
Closing inventory			9,450	9,450		9,450	9,450	
Depreciation charges	4,700				4,700			
Drawings			10,500				10,500	
General expenses	26,081			346	25,735			
Machinery at cost	23,500						23,500	
Machinery accumulated depreciation		7,920						7,920
Opening inventory	8,190				8,190			
Prepayments			346				346	
Purchases	58,484				58,484			
Purchases ledger control		7,368		247				7,615
Rent receivable		2,765				2,765		
Sales		117,622				117,622		
Sales ledger control	13,378						13,378	
Suspense		162	247	85				
Wages	27,084			230	27,314			
Profit/loss for the year					5,414			5,414
TOTAL	170,837	170,837	20,858	20,858	129,837	129,837	66,679	66,679

Tutorial note: the credit balance of £162 on suspense account is cleared by the debit adjustment for £247 and the credit adjustment for £85.